WHAT'S *THIS* GOT TO DO WITH *GOLF?*

THE GOLF TEACHINGS OF THE LATE SEÑOR FRANCISCO LOPEZ VOL. II

Jonathan Fine

Published by Stand Tall International Inc.
3100 Steeles Ave. West
Suite 300
Vaughan, Ontario
L4K 3R1

(905) 760-1800 or 1-888-FINEDEO (phone)
(905) 760-0050 or 1-888-CONDO55 (fax)

Printed and distributed by
Brown Book Company (BBC) Limited
720 King Street West
5th Floor
Toronto, Ontario
M5V 2T3

(416) 504-9696 or 1-800-463-5432 (phone)
(416) 594-9393 (fax)

Printed in Canada

ISBN 0-9681 882-1-4

CONTENTS

Chapter   **Pages**

INTRODUCTION

1.	Introduction	2-4
2.	Who Was Señor Francisco (Frank) Lopez?	5-7
3.	What's *This* Got To Do With *Golf*?	8-11
4.	Having an Open Mind Doesn't Mean That Stuff Will Leak Out	14-17
5.	Thomas Edison to the First Tee, Please!	18-19
6.	Does Your Brain Have Life, Awareness and Consciousness?	20-21
7.	The Needle	22-24
8.	Men and Women Are Different [Duh]	25-27
9.	It's a Trick	28-32
10.	There Is So Much We Don't Know We Don't Know	33-34
11.	Is Mercury, Cheese, a Tiger or a Metal?	35-37
12.	Déjà Vu	38-40
13.	The Bottom Line: Believe It!	41
14.	Golf's Five *Fundamental* Decisions	42-43

COMMITMENT

15.	Are You Committed to Playing the Best Golf That You Can Possibly Play?	46
16.	Is Your Brain Intelligent?	47-48
17.	A Blatant Act of Commitment	49-51
18.	A Commitment Is a *Passionate* Statement	52-53
19.	Suck *IT* in	54-56
20.	Destiny Is Where You Want to Be	57

Chapter   # Pages

21.   Dive in and Get Wet   58
22.   Multiple Choice Quiz   59
23.   Why Are You Surprised?   60
24.   What Are You, a One, Two,   61-64
      Three, Four of Five?
25.   One, Two, Three, Four or Five Golfer   65-68
26.   How Thick Is A Thought?   69-70
27.   Ways You Can vs. Reasons Why You Can't   71-72
28.   Who Is the Best Putter in the World?   73

PLAYING VS. PRACTICING

29.   Are You Playing or Practicing?   76-77
30.   The Question Is the Answer   78
31.   Practice Purposefully and Excellently   79-80
32.   Ph. D (Wedge)   81-82
33.   FG1, G1, FG2, G2, FS1   83-84
34.   Six Pars is an 84   85
35.   The Five Hardest Shots   86
36.   Play the Ladies' Tees   87
37.   Play a Completely Different Game   88
38.   Mental Practice: Your Brain Is a Muscle,   89-90
      Exercise It.

GETTING THE BALL INTO THE HOLE
IN THE FEWEST NUMBER OF STROKES

39.   How Can I Get the Ball into the Hole   92-94
      in the Fewest Number of Strokes?
40.   Use One More Club   95
41.   Putting: Your *Coup De Grace*   96-97
42.   If It's Your Day, the Putts Will Drop   98

Chapter   Pages

43.	This Is a Putt I Make All of the Time	99
44.	Every Putt Is Makeable in Many Different Ways	100
45.	Advice on Getting out of the Woods	101
46.	Nervous on the First Tee	102
47.	If You Are Going to Play Safe, Play Safe!	103-104
48.	Bring it to a Grinding Halt	105-106
49.	The Pre-shot Routine	107-108
50.	Your Lover or a Temptress?	109

MAINTAINING YOUR COMMITMENT

51.	How Are You Going to Maintain Your Commitment Regardless of Whatever Happens on the Golf Course?	112
52.	Head in the Right Direction	113
53.	A Journey of 1,000 Miles Starts with a Single Step	114
54.	Be Good = Feel Good = Think Good = Feel Good = Be Good	115-117
55.	Using the Needle	118-119
56.	Words and Ideas Can Be Barriers and Prisons: What's Your Handicap?	120-121
57.	Fear and Hope Are the Same Thing	122-123
58.	Helicopter Words	124-126
59.	Needle Stopping Words	127-128
60.	Muddle Your Way Around the Course	129-130
61.	Excellence and Integrity	131
62.	Thomas Edison Was A Failure (Until He Succeeded)	132-133
63.	Every Shot Is an Opportunity for Greatness	134-136
64.	Yabbit	137-138
65.	But Yeah	139

Chapter   # Pages

66. Exception or Rule   140
67. What's the Matador Got to Do with Golf?   141-142
68. Look the Bull in the Eyes   143-144
69. Defining Moments   145
70. Wish upon a Par   146
71. Been There? Done That? So Do *IT* Again!   147-148
72. A Picture Is Worth 1,000 Words,   149-151
     Maybe 1,000,000, or More
73. Computer Games   152
74. I Made a Mistake. So What!   153
75. Picking up vs. Giving up   154
76. 'Til Death Do You Part   155
77. The Green Is Waiting for You   156
78. The Time Zones of Your Life   157-158
79. Bull Should   159-160
80. Tune Your Spirit   161-162
81. Are *You* Your Handicap?   163
82. The Hawk and the Shark   164-165
83. More Zone   166-167
84. More about Automatic Golfer   168-170
85. What Were You Thinking About?   171-172
86. Feel the Right Club: 173
     Let Yourself Make the Shot
87. Winning   174-175
88. Tiptoe on a Razor Blade   176
89. Sense the Big Picture   177
90. Get out of Your Own Way: 178
     Get Yourself Together
91. You Can't Argue with the Demons   179-180
92. Always Finish with Three *Great* Shots   181
93. Why Do I Fall Apart on the Back Nine?   182-184
94. Play Three Hole Rounds   185-186
95. Fistful of Jell-O: When the Wheels Fall Off   187

Chapter   Pages

96.   Career Round 18th Hole   188-189
97.   Make Your Last Thought a Smile   190
98.   Precision + Discipline = Excellence + Success   191
99.   Clean Your Clubs and Shine Your Putter   192

HAVE FUN

100.   Am I Going to Have Fun Regardless of   194-195
       Whatever Happens on the Golf Course?
101.   How Are You Going to Live Your Life   196-197
       While You Are Waiting to Die?

EPILOGUE

102.   The Last Conversation   200-201
103.   Epilogue   202-203

Special thanks again to my wife *Shelley* and my children *Corby,
Jamie, Jory* and *Jake*; to my parents *Addy and Bert*; to *Frankie
Lopez* and *the Emilio Lopez family*, to my business partners and
friends *Bob Brown* and *Mario Deo*, and to friends *Pauline Kelly,
Marlene Streit, Cathy Sherk, Steve Justein, Brian Hennick,
Albert Doria, Ken Shaw, Ralph Gileno, Sheldon Sturrock, Peter
Kirsch, Ken Bearg, Phillip Taylor, Dudley Jones, Jim Walker,
Scott Musmanno, Jules Beauregard, Bill Hushion, Dave
Burdick, Don Kramer, David Medhurst, Bob Manion, Chapters
Books, Indigo Books* for their encouragement and support and to
Paula Pike for her editorial advice.

Graphic images contained in the following commercial packages:

Presentation Task Force, Publisher's Task Force, by New Vision
Technologies Inc.; *Word Perfect Suite 7, Corel Gallery, Corel Mega
Gallery, Corel Gallery 3* by Word Perfect Corporation; *PC Paintbrush
Clip Art Collection*, by *SoftKey International Inc.; ClickArt 125,000
Deluxe Image Pak* by T/Maker Company

Cover Design: Roy Chua

FOREWORD

*"Most golfers have experienced the
metaphysical side of golf: that unique, spiritual,
mystical and mystifying thing about the game of
golf that Frank Lopez called "IT." Have you?
Golfers who continually excel however, go
beyond simple awareness of IT and tap into this
energy source and use IT. "*

What's *this* book got to do with golf?

EVERYTHING! Within these covers is the
information *you* need to lower your scores and to
maximize your enjoyment of the game of golf. Frank Lopez'
teachings are powerful lessons; about golf and life: classic golf
and life poetry. Ingest, then digest each verse.

What Frank Lopez teaches us about *golf*, is simply how to use
the skills you have to shoot lower scores. That is the art of
playing the game of golf. You already know how to hold the
club and swing it. *What's This Got to Do with Golf?* is about
how to play the game of golf. How refreshing!

To most golfers, the technique of "swing" has become their
paramount objective. Not only has the enjoyment of "play"
been lost, but scores (and frustration levels) have increased. No
driver of any merit thinks about the mechanics of automobile
driving while driving. *What's This Got to Do with Golf?* points
out very clearly how to apply that same logic to playing golf.

What Frank Lopez teaches us about *life* is to live it; *live it with
excellence and humility, and have fun!* Making excellence your
goal leaves room for error and for success. Humility permits
you to accept that there's a universe of information that you

don't even know you don't know. Open your mind to amazing possibilities. *Why not?*

I first met Jonathan Fine in February, 1997 at the *Toronto Golf and Travel Show*. Due to a burdensome schedule, I was not keen on attending, but an inner voice persuaded me to attend and to assist my friend John Novosel, who was exhibiting his invention, *The Excelerator*. Seemingly by chance, John and I met Jonathan, who was kind enough to autograph copies of his book, *Golf Is A Very Simple Game* for us. That evening, John Novosel was leafing through the book and said to me over and over again, *"Ben, you wrote this book."* As he read passages from the book to me, there were tears in my eyes.

No, I didn't write *Golf Is A Very Simple Game*, but I might as well have written it because I have been teaching it for years. I never met Frank Lopez personally, but I knew him. Frank Lopez and I were brothers: spiritual twins. Every golfer of any merit "knows" Frank Lopez.

Now, in *What's This Got To Do With Golf? The Golf Teachings Of The Late Señor Francisco Lopez, Vol. II*, Jonathan Fine has taken golf books to the next level. Most golfers have experienced the metaphysical side of golf: that unique, spiritual, mystical and mystifying thing about the game of golf that Frank Lopez called "IT." *Have you?* Golfers who continually excel however, go beyond simple awareness of IT and tap into this energy source and use IT.

What's this got to do with golf?

"IT" is golf! Read it, study it, and then you'll live "IT."

Ben Jackson
Golf Professional
Stonington Country Club
Stonington, CT
January, 1999

INTRODUCTION

1

INTRODUCTION

*"As the summer wore on, this same hawk
always seemed to be there when something good
(and weird) happened."*

---

*W*eird things began happening to me two days after
Frank Lopez died.

Waking before dawn, I was startled by a satiny,
gossamer-like cloud of energy pulsating near an electrical outlet
in my home! Like a dull flashbulb,
it lasted only for a moment, but for
that moment, I felt a distinctly eerie
and powerful presence. *It was Frank!*
I have since felt that presence many
times.

Exactly two weeks and two days
earlier, Frank told me what his
doctors had told him: *he had two
weeks to live.* During the next two
weeks, we talked openly and frankly
about life, and about his impending
death. Strangely enough, our discussions
were *not* somber. We even *joked* that he
would come back to visit me after he had died
and help me with my game! *And I believe
that he did!*

Three weeks after Frank died I birdied the first hole of the golf
season by chipping in from the fringe of the green. I couldn't

help looking over my shoulder. In the still-barren trees of early spring, I *first* noticed the hawk that now frequents our course. As the summer wore on, this same hawk always seemed to be there when something good (and weird) happened, which by the way, happened throughout that season with unusual frequency. A holed-out bunker shot that took a sharp left turn as it hit the green and flew into the cup; a 160-yard shot for an eagle; a 5-wood into a par three that landed in the cup (but alas did not see fit to remain there), and many more.

About the same time, I became inexplicably obsessed with the investigation of expanding one's consciousness, awareness and understanding, out of which grew my personal motivation seminar which I called *Stand Tall, Be Proud and Hit It*, of course dedicated to my friend Frank Lopez.

Then, with what I thought was a view to improving my golf, I began to compile on my word processor, the information that Frank left me[1]. Eventually, as words turned into sentences, sentences into paragraphs and paragraphs into chapters, I realized that I was in fact writing a book. Me, writing a book! More than once I have re-read portions of *Golf Is a Very Simple Game: The*

---

[1]   Frank and I had discussed making an infomercial of his teachings, but his imminent death would make that impossible. Instead, quite apart from 20 years of teaching, Frank's dying legacy to me was a set of audio tapes that he had dictated for me, containing his final reflections on life, death and golf.

Golf Teachings of the Late Señor Francisco Lopez[2] and questioned whether in fact I was the author, or merely the typist. There were times when I would simply put my fingers on the keyboard, relax and watch with amazement at what was produced.

As a matter of fact, it continues even today!

---

[2]   *Golf Is a Very Simple Game. The Golf Teachings of the Late Señor Francisco Lopez* is the fist volume of this series of books authored by Mr. Fine.

2

WHO WAS SEÑOR
FRANCISCO (FRANK) LOPEZ?

*"There is something unique, spiritual, mystical
and mystifying about the game of golf ("IT")
that you don't find in any other sport. In order to
achieve your full potential as a golfer and to obtain the
maximum enjoyment, it is critical that you be aware of
IT. Believe that IT is true and then experience IT, live
IT, play IT and LOVE IT."*

*F*rank Lopez was probably nobody *you've* heard of, but
he was *my* golf teacher and my *friend.*

As a golf teacher, Frank gave me a passion for the
game of golf and the notion that golf was
fun. At a deeper level and in a subtle
way, Frank's message was that there is
something unique, spiritual, mystical and
mystifying about the
game of golf[1] ("IT"[2])

---

[1]   And life.

[2]   It is important for the reader to note that in his conversations
with me, Frank Lopez actually gave the word "IT" *a much
wider meaning*, including, achieving greatness on the golf
course, the energy of the universe, the human energy field,
the course of destiny and much more, *all of which Frank*

that you don't find in any other sport. In order to achieve your full potential as a golfer and to obtain the maximum enjoyment, it is critical that you be aware of IT. Believe that IT is true and then experience IT, live IT, play IT and LOVE IT.

As a friend, Frank taught me about life, and death, and then much more. In fact, it was not until people started telling me that *Golf Is a Very Simple Game* was really a book about *life lessons* as much about golf lessons, that I realized what Frank *had really been teaching me* in our many conversations over the previous 20 years! Strangely enough, many of these conversations seemingly had nothing to do with golf. The deeper I've investigated, however, the more I've understood the connection. *And it's quite amazing.*

It's difficult for me to imagine what a person thinks about knowing that he or she is going to die in a matter of days. It is said that some gain an insight - as if receiving a glimpse of a different existence. In Frank's case, he became philosophical in a manner not previously demonstrated to me - as if his personal wisdom and view of the universe had been supplemented with some kind of revelation.

believed were connected. Therefore, if the usage of the defined term "IT" does not seem to make immediate sense, the reader is invited to consider the particular usage thereof within the context of the overall philosophy of life and golf which embraces the various themes in this book.

Then suddenly,
all of this knowledge distilled to a point

and exploded.

3

WHAT'S *THIS* GOT TO DO WITH *GOLF*?

"YOU can improve YOUR golf just by changing the way that YOU think."

I suspect you may be asking yourself whether this author really believes that the spirit of a virtually unknown and now dead golf pro somehow helped him play better golf.

For the record, I do, but whether it's true or not doesn't matter because *as a result of this belief, my golf improved dramatically, just by changing the way that I thought. Just by changing my beliefs.*

Let that sink in for a minute because it's the point of this book. *YOU can improve YOUR golf just by changing the way that YOU think.* I know that you can do it, because I did it and I'm just like you.

Not to bore you with my meager achievements, but in each one of my four club championship matches the summer that I was writing *Golf Is a Very Simple Game*, once again *something good and weird happened* at a critical time in each match. How about chipping in on the 18th for the first-round match. In the quarter-finals, it was a first-hole lob-wedge birdie that turned my opponent to mush. In the finals, a drained 40-footer on the first hole gave me control of the match.

The most striking occurrence, however, was during the 16th hole of the semi-final match. Standing on the 16th tee, the best that I had stood to that point was even.[1] This par-four hole appears from the tee to be one of the easier holes. Apparently WYSIWYG[2], but the golfer is not aware of the subtle nuances until one's 2nd shot, which one discovers is usually taken from anything but a flat lie. Quite apart from a fairway reminiscent of the slanted floor of a midway's fun house, one has to consider a series of sand and grass bunkers which corral the green, the undulating mounds which flank these bunkers, a small forest and *one solitary fir tree*, 37 paces in front of and to the right of the flagstick. My second shot found its way under that tree.

"Great #*&)#@!!! shot, Jon. You fight back from three down, get a chance to get back to even and then you do this. Look at that $%(*&@#) ball. You're going to have to stand with that branch between your legs. What the heck should I hit?"

Having asked *myself* the question, I didn't really expect to get an answer, but I swear to you that I heard a familiar Spanish-accented voice say, *"Juan, hit a 7-iron!"*

You really had to see this. Standing in the midst of that fir tree, straddling a branch which protruded perilously through my legs, unable to see all of the ball, I hit a 7-iron *just as Frank had*

---

[1]   On the first tee.

[2]   For the techno-challenged "What You See Is What You Get."

instructed me to do! The ball popped out of the
tree, rolled down one side of the grass bunker
and up the other side, through the double-
cut fringe, onto the green, hit the flagstick
and came to rest about an inch from the hole!
Needless to say, my opponent three-putted from about
12 feet and the match was even, and then mine to win on
the 18th.   To this day, he maintains that he was
distracted by the screech of a hawk.

Taken as *unrelated* events, it's easy to explain these
occurrences simply as four lucky shots at critical times in
each match, coincidence or perhaps just as things that
happen to someone who plays a lot of golf. On the other
hand, someone who believes that he is receiving
assistance from the spirit of a dead golf pro may just
believe that these events are *interrelated.* The point is
however, that *it doesn't matter* whether or not these are
interrelated events, because *how would we ever know
anyway?*

> ### *What matters is
> whether you BELIEVE
> IT COULD BE possible.*

What's *this* got to do with *golf*?

If you are open to the *possibility* that maybe you *don't know*
everything there is to know about everything, *even about things
that you don't know you don't know,* then you may be able to
improve your golf.

An open mind and belief are fundamental to reaching your next golfing level and your full potential as a golfer. And I'll tell you why soon. In my case, whether Frank Lopez' "spirit" *actually* appeared near an electrical outlet in my home two days after he died is something that I will never know for sure. Being open to the possibility that it might have happened has opened up a whole new world of *possibilities* to me,

and best of all, my golf improved!

Jonathan Fine

February, 1999

WHAT'S *THIS* GOT TO DO WITH *GOLF?*

4

HAVING AN OPEN MIND DOESN'T MEAN THAT STUFF WILL LEAK OUT

"Golfers who have an open mind understand perfectly that the object of the game of golf is to get the ball into the hole in the fewest number of strokes, and then they find imaginative ways to do so hole after hole after hole."

J uan[1], I am going to tell you some things that you may have trouble believing or understanding right away, but you've got to have an open mind. Don't be afraid. Trust me. Having an open mind doesn't mean that stuff will leak out.

Most people go through their lives with a closed mind. New ideas and their *perpetrators* are met with cynicism, criticism and derision. Perpetrators of new ideas are labeled

[1] As in *Golf is a Very Simple Game: The Golf Teachings of the Late Señor Francisco Lopez*, the balance of Volume II is a lightly edited transcription of the tapes and ideas given to me by Frank interspersed with my remembrances of his teachings, the many conversations that I had with him over almost 20 years and my thoughts. Although the book is written as Frank speaking to me (he called me "Juan") , I have chosen not to use quotation marks.

radicals, crack-pots, fools and cranks until a *new* idea is generally recognized as a *good* idea, and then do you know what we call them?

[Radicals, crack-pots, fools and cranks?]

We call them geniuses, inventors, scientists, brilliant, innovators, etc.

[Hmmm.]

Are you a cynic, Juan?

["Cynic" has too much of a bite to it.   I would say that I am a passive judgmental observer.]

It's easy to be a cynic. Cynicism is caused by having a closed mind, which insulates you from any new ideas. Cynics look for negativity and for reasons why not.

[What's *this* got to do with *golf*?]

Golfers who don't improve are cynics. They have a closed mind to new ideas and are quite comfortable *playing as badly as they have always played*, and even worse. Sometimes, they play up to what they believe their best game to be, and then the cynicism kicks in, preventing them from climbing above their self-imposed ceilings.

On the other hand, golfers who have an open mind understand *perfectly* that the object of the game of golf is to get the ball into the hole in the fewest number of strokes, and then they find imaginative ways to do this hole after hole after hole. *They see each shot as a unique, beautiful and wondrous event.* Every shot is a culmination of decisions based upon numerous factors present at that precise moment. *These golfers are not constrained by the artificial concepts of "par" and "handicap",* and not only give themselves *permission* to succeed and improve, but strive to do so round after round after round. These golfers believe that parring, even birdieing every hole is possible and set out to achieve IT, somehow, someway, whatever IT takes. At the end of a round, the score is merely the number of strokes taken to get the ball into the hole 18 times and is not an artificial and limiting judgmental definition of their ability.

You have a choice.
You can have

an open mind   OR   a closed mind.

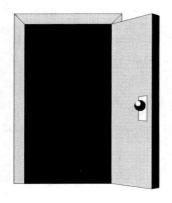 

It's YOUR choice.

**Keep the door open, Juan,
      you never know what may come through.**

*You can pick and choose
      what you want to use.
            If you have a closed mind
                  you can't, and you lose.*

*Having an open mind
doesn't mean that stuff will leak out.*

5

THOMAS EDISON
TO THE FIRST TEE, PLEASE!

"We still don't know one-millionth of 1 percent of anything"

---

*D*o you know who Thomas Edison was?

[Sure. If he hadn't invented the light bulb, we would have to watch TV in the dark.]

Thomas Edison said:

"We don't know one-millionth of 1 percent of anything."

[.000001 percent! I think Tom was probably just exaggerating to make the point.]

Think about that for a minute. According to Thomas Edison, of all of the stuff there is to know, he thought that we don't know 99.999999 percent of it. Do you think Edison was correct? What do you think?

[Well, let's see. Edison was born in 1847 and died in 1931. Thinking of the modern advances in technology, science, medicine, space travel, computers, etc., .000001 percent just can't be correct today. But how can I assign a percentage if I don't know what 100 percent is?]

Do you know what Thomas Edison would say if he were alive today?

[I'm the oldest man in history?]

He'd say *"We <u>still</u> don't know one-millionth of 1 percent of anything."*

[What's *this* got to do with *golf*?]

Maybe, just maybe, there's something that you don't even know you don't know that could improve your golfing performance and enjoyment!

Reserve the right to be smarter today than you were yesterday.

6

DOES YOUR BRAIN HAVE LIFE, AWARENESS AND CONSCIOUSNESS?

"Energy. Invisible energy, Juan. The universe is filled with invisible energy. More forces than you could imagine."

Does your brain have life, awareness and consciousness?

[I'll bet you'll say no.]

You're right. Your brain is made up of living cells, but it does not have *life* in the sense that I mean. Your brain has no awareness or consciousness. There *is* something about *you* that *does* have life, that is aware and conscious, but it is not your brain.

[You are losing me.]

Close your eyes and think about this. Imagine your body. Now, one at a time, take away the flesh, muscles, bones, nerves, blood and organs part of you from the rest. What is left?

[A mess?]

Once you get rid of the physical

part, what's left is the real "YOU" - your ideas, experiences, likes, dislikes, preferences, prejudices, opinions, conscience, morals, principles, etc. In other words, what YOU call "YOUR IDENTITY" is really the sum total of your life experiences.

You can't remember this, but try to think back to who YOU were when you were born. There was a clean slate. In terms of your ideas, experiences, likes, dislikes, preferences, prejudices, opinions, conscience, morals, principles, etc., there was no YOU. It was like a blank piece of paper. Then, as things happened, what YOU call "ME" began to take shape, like a shell. As a matter of fact, what YOU call "ME" is continuing to take shape even as you listen to this.

Now, if you strip away that bundle of experiences called "YOU", what remains?

[A new born baby minus the baby?]

Energy. Invisible energy, Juan. *The universe is filled with invisible energy.* More forces than you can imagine. I know this now. *For the time being*, this energy is resident in and energizing a mushy biological computer (yours). This *energy* uses your body to nourish, transport and protect the computer until your body can't or doesn't do it anymore and *then the energy leaves and goes somewhere else.*

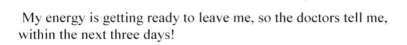

 My energy is getting ready to leave me, so the doctors tell me, within the next three days!

7

THE NEEDLE

"You can take these ideas, if you choose, and use them to make your light burn brighter and stronger and live your life with greater intensity."

Many years ago I visited a spiritual man who showed me that there is something about the human body, an invisible energy, that can cause metal to move!

[Was his name Don Juan Matus by any chance?]

Are you at least open to the possibility that what he showed me falls into Edison's 99.9999999 percent of things that we don't know anything about? Are you open to the possibility that the human body generates invisible energy that can cause metal to move?

[No, and can we please get back to the golf part?]

You are *very* skeptical and cynical, and you are probably thinking that the cancer has hit my brain. I know it's difficult for you to believe, but there has been enough taught and written over the last 4000 years about some form of human energy field or whatever you want to call IT[1] that one would be foolish to dismiss the idea outright. Eastern civilizations have *used* this knowledge to improve the quality of their lives. In fact, our North American culture is perhaps the only culture that *actively denies and suppresses* information about the human energy field.

Do you know what *Chi* is?

[Part of the name of a golfer of Spanish descent who more than 10 people have ever heard of?]

Chi is a Chinese word and concept that means energy. It is said that everything, living or inanimate, has its own *Chi;* its own energy field. Your *Chi* circulates through your body however, IT is not something that you touch, feel or see, but rather something that you sense the existence of as a result of being aware of how you feel. IT can be transferred from one person to another and even from one  object to another. The intensity of your *Chi* can vary according to what you eat, think and experience. *Chi* is a mysterious thing and for the average person of Western upbringing, this elementary explanation is satisfactory, but it just touches the true meaning of *Chi.*

There are also those that believe that the human existence is marked by a fleshy body and a body of light that travel together although not exactly within the same spatial co-ordinates or even in the same realm of existence. It is said that this body of light

---

[1]   *Chi, élan vital, anima,* life force, etc.

is the "real" you, connected to a universal awareness. Your
fleshy body is just a *temporary* home.

[Frank, that can't be true.]

Who knows? How would we ever know if any of this is *"true"*?
Whether these things are true or not just doesn't
matter. *What does matter* is that you can take these
ideas, if you choose, and *use* them to make your
light burn brighter and stronger *and live
your life with greater intensity.* Or,
                              you can
                              reject
these ideas as stupid, or impossible,
and do nothing.

[How about some golf stuff?]

MEN AND WOMEN
ARE DIFFERENT
[DUH]

"This is golf stuff and probably the most important thing I can teach you."

ow about some golf stuff? This is golf stuff and probably the most important thing I can teach you. Let me show you what I discovered when I did some further experiments of my own. Move that chair in front of this mirror, sit down with your feet apart, your hands on your thighs and watch what I do. Leave me room to stand behind you. What I'm holding over your head is a sewing needle hanging from a piece of thread. Just sit still for a few seconds, I have to find the right spot. Okay, now what is happening to the needle?

[It's spinning in a circle.]

Yes, it is spinning in a counter-clockwise circle. That's because you are a man.

[I think I knew that already, but thank you for reassuring me.]

Don't be a smart aleck. If you were a woman, the needle would spin *clockwise*.

[Excuse me?]

Counter-clockwise for a man, clockwise for a woman. You may have heard of this, how you call it, "old lady's story[1]" about predicting the sex of unborn babies?

[Yeah, I saw someone do that once. But if you did this in Australia, would the needle spin in the opposite directions? What about at the equator?]

I don't know Juan, because I've never been to Australia or to the equator, but watch this. Take your hands off your thighs, and touch your fingertips together forming a steeple. What's happening?

[The needle is starting to spin the other way. Yikes.]

Put your hands back on your thighs. Now what?

[The needle is starting to spin counter-clockwise again. Yikes.]

Now watch this. I want you to think about the most exciting thought that you can possibly think of. Something that sends chills up and down your spine. Something that you know would make you feel the best that you could possibly feel. What's happening to the needle?

[It's spinning like a helicopter. Wow! Look at that thing go!]

---

[1]   Old wives' tale.

Now I want you to think about the worst, most depressing thing
that could ever happen to you. Imagine and feel it vividly.
Good. Now, what's happening?

[It's stopped spinning.   It's just hanging there!]

IT'S A TRICK

*"It works if you believe it works. You don't
need to know why. Whether all this is true or
not, just doesn't matter to me. The only thing
that matters is whether I believe it's true. ...
And, golf is a game of perception, belief and
attitude. Not a game of truth."*

So what do you think Juan, do you believe what you've just seen is true?

[I don't think so.]

You think I was tweaking my
fingers, causing the needle to spin,
don't you? You think it's a trick.

[The thought had crossed my mind.]

It's not a trick and I wasn't consciously
causing the needle to spin. From a dying
man, you better believe it.

[So what causes the needle to
spin?]

Before I explain that, let me tell you some more things that I
discovered on my own. The needle will spin over other points on
the body, called *chakra* points. If you don't *hold* the thread, but
just *hang* it (for example from a stretched thread), the needle
will *not* spin. It only seems to work with a person holding it.

[Do you really believe all this is true?]

I *do not know* whether what I have showed you is the "truth". I *do know* that I am *not* consciously causing the needle to spin, but on the other hand, I cannot prove or explain *The Needle*.[1]

What causes the needle to spin *might* be an electromagnetic force field, a human energy field, some yet undiscovered phenomenon caused by the interaction between two persons' electromagnetic force fields, something that we don't have a name for yet, something we don't even have the capacity to understand *or the words in our vocabulary* to explain accurately. I know that *I* don't have the time in this life to wait for the *truth*. What I *also* know is that by simply approaching this subject with an open mind and a sense of wonderment, I have satisfied myself (at least to the degree that I have been able to use effectively in my life) as to the existence of what I *believe* to be a human energy field!

So, do I believe? I do have my own theory which is that we have an energy field that varies with intensity according to our thoughts and emotions. Furthermore, among the thousands of types of invisible energy, there are two fundamental energies: a "female" energy and a "male" energy.

I can also tell you without any hesitation, that through my experiments with *The Needle*, I have also satisfied myself that one's thoughts can influence (not predict or manipulate) events, alter experiences and create whatever reality one chooses. I *don't know* why, I *don't know* how. I *do know* that it occurs. This observation, taken as fact, has incredibly powerful potential. In

---

[1]   He began calling this demonstration "The Needle".

other words, it works if you believe it works. You don't need to
know why. Whether all this is *true* or not, just *doesn't matter to
me. The only thing that matters is whether I believe it's true.*

Let me say it again because it's important.

The "truth" simply doesn't matter.
What matters is what I believe the truth to be.

Belief and faith are more powerful than we can even imagine.
Moreover, belief and faith *by a group of people*
is exponentially more powerful. I used to look
with amazement at TV programs
about ordinary people who, when in
a group setting, participate in healing.
I listened with interest to the ordinary
people who conducted this healing say
things like *"It works. If you don't believe
that it works, then you don't know what you
are missing."* I now understand what they
were saying.

So, Juan, do you believe?

DO YOU BELIEEEEEEEEEEEEEEVE?

[Frank, what's *this* got to do with golf?]

We *shape our lives* by what we *believe* to be true. We act
according to our beliefs. We have very little knowledge about
truth. If Edison is correct, the best we could hope to *know* is
000001 percent of the "truth", but life goes on according to what
we believe. In your life, if you wait to act until you discover the
truth, the absolute truth, I suspect you are going to do a lot of
sitting around doing nothing.

In golfing terms, if you wait until your swing is perfect and you are a four handicap before you decide that you are ready (or worthy) to *play* golf, you are going to waste a lot of time. You can't even sign your name exactly the same way twice in a row, how are you going to duplicate the perfect golf swing?

On the other hand, you might want to consider what philosophers, writers about the human condition, motivators and sports psychologists have been telling those who would listen: *you have the ability to change the quality of our life just by thinking.* You've heard the expression "perception is reality." Well, it means a lot of different things, but most importantly it means that you can create your own reality, *just by thinking IT!*

You can create your own reality, *just by thinking IT!*

And, golf is a game of perception, belief and attitude

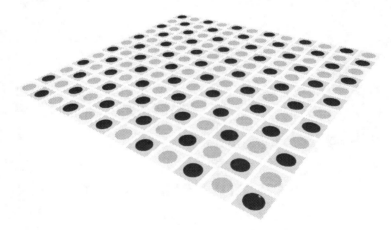

Not a game of truth.

[?]

10

THERE IS SO MUCH
WE DON'T KNOW
WE DON'T KNOW

"The only thing that matters is what we believe to be true because we act according to our beliefs."

id you know that under certain circumstances, if the end of a young child's finger is cut off, it will grow back perfectly in a matter of months?[1]

[That's really going to help me break 80!]

[1]   Much to my surprise, I subsequently confirmed this in *The Body Electric*, Robert O. Becker, M.D., and Gary Selden, 1985, William Morrow and Company Inc.

"Young children's fingers cleanly sheared off beyond the outermost crease of the outermost joint will invariably regrow perfectly in about three months. This crease seems to be a sharp dividing line, with no intermediate zone between perfect restoration and none at all. ... A lost one will regenerate as good as new, whereas one that has merely been mutilated will heal as a stump or with heavy scarring."

33

There is so much *we don't know* we don't know.

[Can you say that again that again?]

There is so much we don't know we don't know. The best that we can hope to do is to try to *understand* what we *observe* within the *limitations* of our *language* and the extent of our present understanding of the universe, and then try to *use* what we *believe* to be true to enrich our lives.

[Would you say that again in plain English, please?]

The only thing that matters is what we believe to be true because we act according to our beliefs.

11

IS MERCURY, CHEESE, A TIGER OR A METAL?

"It doesn't matter whether it's possible or impossible. ... What matters is whether you believe it could be possible."

B *ack to The Needle. Do you believe it's true?*

[It can't be true. There's no way that there's an invisible energy about our bodies that can cause metal to move. No way!]

Let me give you an example my cynical, close-minded friend who apparently has *not* been listening to anything that I have been talking about. Let's say you have been jogging on a cold winter's day, and after about 30 minutes, you take your gloves off. What are you going to see?

[My hands?]

Steam, Juan, Steam. Then, you put your gloves back on and you run for another 30 minutes and go inside. As soon as you go inside, you take your gloves off, cup your hands together and someone puts a thermometer between your cupped hands without touching them. What's going to happen to the mercury in the thermometer?

[It will rise.]

Of course it will rise. What causes the mercury to move inside the thermometer?

[I can see this coming. Heat.]

Riiiight. Now Juan, answer me these two
questions:

Is heat an invisible energy associated
with the body?

[Yes, Frank.]

Is mercury,
cheese, a tiger or a metal?

[Hmmm.]

See what I'm getting at?

[Interesting.]

Can you accept that the fact that heat is invisible energy
produced by the body which can cause the mercury in a
thermometer to move?

[I guess I've known that since I was a kid.]

So if the human body can generate that type of invisible energy
that can cause that metal to move, why can't there be another
type of energy which the body produces that causes *The Needle*
to move?

[Because there isn't.]

You are hopeless, Juan. If you do not believe that the human
body generates invisible energy that can cause metal to move,
are you at least *open to the possibility* that such energy *may* exist
but that IT just hasn't been "discovered" yet?

[It's impossible, Frank.]

Impossible is a word that human beings use to explain what they don't, can't or don't want to understand. The point is that it doesn't matter whether it's possible or impossible. How many more times do I have to tell you this? *What matters is whether you believe it could be possible.* What matters is whether *you believe* that by thinking good thoughts you can "brighten" your own energy. What matters is whether *you believe* that by thinking good thoughts you will feel good and be good.

[What's *this* got to do with golf?]

How you perceive yourself, your ability as a golfer, the game of golf and every shot that you make, is directly affected by what you believe and most importantly, by the intensity of your personal energy field. *If you believe that by thinking good thoughts you can "brighten" your own energy,* then you are on your way to playing the best golf that you can possibly play.

12

DÉJÀ VU

"It happens to everyone! Does that tell you something?"

---

*H*ave *you ever had a déjà vu experience?*

[I missed a one-foot putt last week and I was sure that I had done it before. Is that what you mean?]

Juan, I'm serious. Have you ever thought of something and then it happened?

[Yes. Seriously.]

Sure. All of us have had these types of experiences to varying degrees, but most of us keep them to ourselves. As a matter of fact, I have yet to have *anyone* tell me that they have not had some type of "psychic" experience. Juan, it happens to everyone! Does that tell you something?

[I guess *you* should know the answer to that question.]

Have you ever been driving somewhere and mentioned something to your wife and she said

"I was just thinking about that exact same thing."

[Yeah, it happened just the other day.]

Of course you have, because it happens to everybody! Does *that* tell you something?

[Not exactly.]

Maybe we [humans] are at a comparable stage in the evolutionary development of this 6th sense to where we were when we were developing the ability to communicate with language. At that time, although we had the physical equipment (vocal cords, brains, mouths and tongues), *we didn't know how to use it in a meaningful way.* The very first word "spoken" by a human was probably the word "no" ("nah", "neh"), uttered as an involuntary, guttural reaction to an unpleasant event. Eventually however, there must have been one human who *first* realized that he or she had *and could use*, the ability to communicate to another human, his or her ideas through language.

But in evolutionary terms, how long did it take for this realization to develop?

Let's face it, there are phenomena that occur that we cannot yet explain. *But is this situation any different than it was at any other point in time?* No. There have always been occurrences that were not explainable within man's *then current state of understanding* and knowledge. For example, human beings observed apples falling from trees before Newton "discovered" gravity and explained why apples fell down and not up. I suspect that people didn't deny the existence of gravity before it was explained, but for some reason, we tend to deny the existence of unexplainable phenomenon, rather than rejoice. If you are to gain any benefit from these occurrences in your life, Juan, leave "why and how" to others and simply observe "is".

So, Juan:

Are you open to the possibility that there is something about our bodies that causes the needle to spin?

Can you accept that something "is", even if you don't know why, how or what?

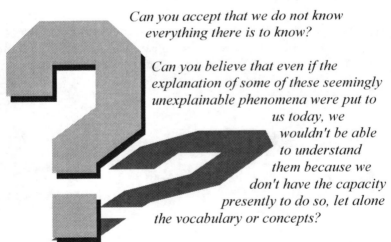

Can you accept that we do not know everything there is to know?

Can you believe that even if the explanation of some of these seemingly unexplainable phenomena were put to us today, we wouldn't be able to understand them because we don't have the capacity presently to do so, let alone the vocabulary or concepts?

Do you go through the journey of life with a closed mind, or an open mind?

The answers to these questions say a lot about how you proceed along the journey of life. The answers to these questions say a lot about how you *play* the *game* of golf.

[?]

THE BOTTOM LINE: BELIEVE IT!

"You can and will play the best golf that you can possibly play."

I know you are thinking to yourself "Frank, what's the bottom line?" There's always got to be a bottom line with you. Is that a lawyer thing? Well here it is.

Golf is a very simple game *if you believe* that IT is a very simple game.

You will play better golf *if you believe* that you will play better golf.

You will have fun playing golf *if you believe* that golf is a game, and that it is possible to have fun regardless of the result.

You will achieve golf greatness *if you believe* that every shot that you make gives you an opportunity for greatness.

You can and you will play the best golf that you can possibly play.

BELIEVE IT!

GOLF'S FIVE FUNDAMENTAL DECISIONS

"We have been talking about real golf stuff!"

I bet you are asking yourself when we are going to get to the *real* golf stuff.

[You read my mind.]

We have been talking about real golf stuff!

{I mean stuff about how to play golf on the course.}

You're not ready for the golf course quite yet because there are five fundamental *decisions* that you have to make before you tee-off. Golf is a game of decisions. A game of actions and consequences. On every shot that you take, I bet that you are making between five to 10 different decisions. For example, how far am I to the flagstick? To the front of the green? To the trouble? Is the wind going to affect my shot? Which club should I use? What type of shot should I hit? High, low, fade, draw? In an 18-hole round, that's a lot of decisions to make.

at the highest level of your ability, then there are the five fundamental decisions that you have to make even *before* you tee-off:

1. Are you *committed* to playing the best golf that you can possibly play?

2. Are you *playing or practicing*?

3. Is your *sole objective* to get the ball into the hole in the fewest number of strokes?

4. Are you going to *maintain your commitment regardless* of whatever happens on the golf course?

5. Are you going to *have fun regardless* of whatever happens on the golf course?

COMMITMENT

15

ARE YOU COMMITTED TO PLAYING THE BEST GOLF THAT YOU CAN POSSIBLY PLAY?

"Decisions are the origin of commitment.
Decisions are one way that you program your mind."

 o you want to improve your game, Juan? Do you want to play the best that you can possibly play?

[Yeah.]

Of course you do, but *how much* do you want to improve? *How good* do you want to be?

[I don't know. I'd like to be a better golfer but I believe that at this point, it will be difficult for me to improve.]

You can and you will improve. The first thing that you must decide is *how good* you want to be. Think about it and state it precisely. For example, do you want to lower your handicap five strokes, do you want to shoot in the 70's or 80's consistently? Whatever your decision is, state it precisely, out loud.

Decisions are the origin of commitment.
Decisions are one way that you program your mind.

46

16

IS YOUR BRAIN INTELLIGENT?

"Your brain is simply a highly sophisticated fleshy biological computer. The way that YOU experience YOUR LIFE is determined by the current state of YOUR COMPUTER'S database and the programs that are currently running."

*I*s you brain intelligent?

[I would hope so. I'm a lawyer, you know.]

I've got some bad news for you. Your brain is not intelligent.

[So, you once gave me a golf lesson that didn't help that much. Big deal. Is this really a productive use of our time?]

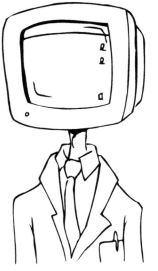

Don't be offended, but your thoughts are simply your brain talking to itself, trying to make sense of the incredible amount of information that it receives every second.

[My brain must be intelligent if it can process all of that information.]

I didn't say it wasn't an incredibly complex organ or not suited for its purpose. It just isn't intelligent. *Your brain is simply a highly sophisticated fleshy biological computer.*

The way that YOU experience YOUR LIFE is determined by the current state of YOUR COMPUTER'S database and the programs that are currently running. Your brain uses all of your past experiences and the judgments that you have made about them, together with your hopes and expectations for the future, as frames of reference to interpret the information that it receives. Then it instantaneously decides what to do with this information.

Your brain is programmed in different ways. One way is by the judgments that you have made about everything that you have ever experienced. You can also consciously program your brain. *The easiest and most subtle way is simply by making a decision.* In other words, you can tell your brain how you want it to process and interpret information that it receives. Beware, however; just like a computer, once you program your mind, you will think and act accordingly. *Our actions flow from our thoughts.*

Your brain is your servant, but once you set it loose, it is your master!

[Can we please get back to how I'm going to improve my golf?]

17

A BLATANT ACT
OF COMMITMENT

*"Writing your goals is an act of commitment
which alerts the forces of the universe that you
are serious about achieving your goals."*

---

 et *back* to how you're going to improve your golf?
That's what we've been talking about.

[?]

Okay, what are your golfing goals this year?

[I want to get better.]

Simply saying "I want to get better" is too
vague. "Getting better" is a matter of
opinion and can't be easily measured.
What you need are *specific* golfing goals.
Your goals must be lofty but realistic. Start
off by setting them just
above what you
believe your peak
performance level
to be. Here are
some specific
golfing goals that
you can aim for
this season. You
fill in the blanks:

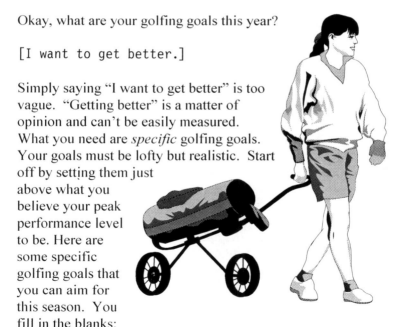

A round with ____ putts

A round hitting ____% of fairways

A round hitting _____% of greens

18 holes with ____ birdies

18 holes with ____ pars

18 holes with ____ bogeys

18 holes with ____ double bogeys

A handicap of _____

Shooting a score of ____

Breaking ____

Tournament Championship.   YES ( )

Make a written declaration of your goals now and keep them taped to your locker at the club or on your golf bag. *If you can't be bothered to even sit down and write your goals, what does that tell you about the intensity of your commitment to be a better golfer?*

It's hard to believe, but if you just make this simple, but *blatant, act of commitment, you will start achieving your goals immediately.*[1]

---

[1]   I followed Frank's advice and the results were spectacular. Of the six goals that I had set for myself, I achieved three of them within a week. My first goal was a round with 29 putts.

Writing your goals is an act of commitment which alerts the forces of the universe

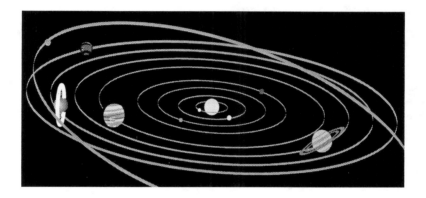

that you are serious about achieving your goals.

My goals were posted conspicuously on my locker door, and I made a point of stating *this* goal prior to playing. I believe that just by doing that, my subconscious seemed to take over and realize that making 29 putts was important to me. I found myself practicing not only my putting, but my chipping too. The result: 18 holes with 27 putts, only 11 on the front nine!

18

A COMMITMENT
IS A *PASSIONATE* STATEMENT

*"When you make that commitment to play the
best golf you can possibly play, it automatically
becomes important to you to play golf well and
you instinctively find ways to do this."*

*A*re you prepared to make the commitment to reach
your goals?

[Yeah, I guess.]

Yeah, I guess? It sounds to me like you're not quite sure or that
you may be telling me what you think I want to
hear. Being committed is for YOU, not for me.
If YOU are not interested in being committed to
playing the best golf that you possibly can,
that's YOUR choice. But, like every other
decision in life, there are consequences. For
example, don't expect your scores to be the
best they can possibly be. *Good scores
don't just happen by accident.*

Being committed to playing
the best golf that you can
possibly play is a passionate
statement - *"I really, really want to play the best golf that I can
possibly play."* It's not *"yeah, I guess."* When you make that
commitment to play the best golf you can possibly play, it
automatically becomes important to you to play golf well and
you *instinctively* find ways to do this.

*Being committed means
that IT is your goal.*

*Think about IT.
Live IT.
Eat IT.
Dream IT.
Breathe IT.
Do IT.*

IT is YOU and YOU are IT.

YOU = IT = YOU = IT

19

SUCK *IT* IN

"YOUR act of commitment is so powerful, it alters and determines the future of the universe."

C ommitment is a powerful display of YOUR connection with the invisible forces of the universe. In fact, YOUR act of commitment is so powerful, it alters and determines the future of the universe. YOU become a witness to evolution.

[Frank, that's a bit of an over-statement, don't you think?]

No I don't. Destiny, more particularly, YOUR DESTINY, is activated and released, simply by making a decision.

[I'm not sure that I understand how, by simply making a decision, my Destiny is activated and released, which changes the future of the universe.]

Being committed is really a decision to move your life in a certain direction. What happens when a truck passes you on the highway?

[Things get sucked in behind it. I think they call it a slipstream.]

The same thing happens to you when you make a decision to move your life in a certain direction, in this case, towards playing the best golf that you can possibly play. The act of commitment, that decision, sets into play a series of actions that reinforce your commitment to play good golf. "Golf things" seem to get attracted to you. In a way that you can't understand *yet*, a course of action is set and a sequence of occurrences begins, *simply by your making a decision.*

[What if these things don't begin to happen?]

They will.
Trust IT! Believe IT!

Take a minute now and ask yourself whether you are committed to playing the best golf that you can possibly play. Really, do it. Say it out loud "*I really, really want to play the best golf that I can possibly play*".

[Am I committed? Yeah! Frank, I really do want to play good golf.]

Shout IT, scream IT, show me you believe IT.

[I REALLY, REALLY WANT TO PLAY THE BEST GOLF THAT I CAN POSSIBLY PLAY. REALLY, REALLY, REALLY!]

[I REALLY, REALLY WANT TO PLAY THE BEST GOLF THAT I CAN POSSIBLY PLAY. REALLY, REALLY, REALLY!]

That's good.

If you really want IT, you'll get IT.

20

DESTINY IS WHERE
YOU WANT TO BE

*"The question is not whether you are going to
change the course of the River Destiny, but
whether you are going to dive into IT."*

T he course of Destiny is unalterably predetermined,
making the future inevitable and irresistible.

[So, then what can I do to change Destiny?]

I'm not asking you to *change* Destiny. I'm
asking you to *live* Destiny. YOUR Destiny.
Destiny is like an invisible river of time, energy
and events. The question is not whether you
are going to change the course of the River
Destiny, but whether you are going to dive
into IT.

Dive In. Get Wet.
Destiny Is
Where YOU Want To Be!

DIVE IN AND GET WET

"Are you going to LIVE until you die?"

Dive in and get wet. That's been my philosophy of life. For me, that's the only way to live. I lived my life this way because I always knew that someday I was going to die, but until recently I didn't know when.

The River Destiny is also the River of Your Life. You're either in or you're out. Standing on the shore, dipping your toes while you decide whether to dive in, means you are out. If you're committed, you're in. All the way. Yes, you get wet, you might get cold, you might drown. *But what's wrong with being soaked with Life?* If the water is cold, you'll get used to it. Everyone is going to die some day. The question: *Are you going to LIVE until you die?* I decided early in my life that when I die, I want to be sure that I had lived Life, not merely watched it go by.

Diving in always commits you.

Fully and Instantly.

MULTIPLE CHOICE QUIZ:

"Are you a player?"

 nswer the following multiple choice quiz:

( ) *ARE YOU A PLAYER?*

OR

( )   *ARE YOU A CADDIE?[1]*

---

[1]   Answer to multiple choice quiz: You are correct!

WHY ARE YOU SURPRISED?

"You couldn't believe that you were the cause of such a good score and attributed your success to luck. But how could IT have been luck when you did IT?"

I remember one day when we played golf and you shot your best score by four strokes. You told me that you were surprised. Do you remember what I said to you?

[Nice game?]

I asked you, *"Why are you surprised?"*

You said to me, *"Because I'm not that good."*

Of course you were that good.
If you weren't that good, you wouldn't have been able to shoot that score. *I* knew you were that good. I also knew that *you* didn't believe that you were that good. *You didn't believe IT.* You were surprised because you had exceeded what you believed your ability to be. You couldn't believe that you were the cause of such a good score and attributed your success to luck. But how could IT have been luck when *you* did IT? YOU caused the ball to get into the hole. YOU were that good.

Why is it that you couldn't believe IT?

WHAT ARE YOU, A ONE, TWO, THREE, FOUR OR FIVE?

"Life is a breeze; let's have some fun; what time do you want to tee-off today? I'm free all day."

---

hat are you, a One, Two, Three, Four or Five?

[How should I know? I wear number five on my hockey sweater, is that what you mean?]

No. I'm going to describe to you five different types of people and how they travel the River of Life. Figure out how you would rate yourself. The five types of people are Ones, Twos, Threes, Fours and Fives.

ONES

Ones go through Life with a flutter board between their legs which causes them to flip upside down. Not only do they have their heads in the water and their feet in the air, they are also trying to paddle, upside down with the paddle sticking out of the water. Their number one thought is *survival. How am I going to get my next breath?*

These people drown very quickly in the River of Life.

TWOS

Twos have discovered the boat, but their boat is water logged with a million holes in it. Did you see the movie *Papillon*? A boat like that. Twos alternate between bailing and paddling. They move forward about an inch a day. They row in circles and last until their strength gives out. Every day for them is a struggle. Their number one thought is *how tired I am;*

how will I make it through the day? what a struggle this is; Life is treating me so badly; Life is so hard; I feel so sorry for myself.

THREES

Threes are the canoeists, the paddlers. They represent 80 per cent of the population. The more you put in, the more you get out. The harder and longer you paddle, the farther you get. Solid work ethic. Point them in the right direction and they will do the job for you. They've got a wide range of ability and as they get closer to the Fours, you even see some of them being creative. The problem is, they have no time. Their number one thought is still on *the*

mechanics of paddling. They live their lives *shoulda, coulda, woulda.*

FOURS

Fours start to approach the realm of the superstars. The Fours drive a motor boat. They've got one hand on the motor and they're making notes with the other.

They're planning. They're being creative. They're using their minds. They don't have to think about the mechanics of what they are doing. Start their boat and it goes. The Four's number one thought is, *"I see the pot of gold at the end of the rainbow, now I have to figure out how to get it?*

FIVES

Who are these people? These are the people who have other people driving their yachts. They've got lots of time to do anything that they want to do. Fives are thinking, ***"Life is a breeze; let's have some fun; what time do you want to tee-off today? I'm free all day."***

WHAT ARE YOU?[2]

---

[2]   Readers are urged to actually (and honestly) figure out how you would rate yourself according to this scale, and then circle the appropriate number above.

ONE, TWO, THREE, FOUR, FIVE GOLFER

"What type of golfer are you?"

W *hat type of golfer are you, a One, Two, Three, Four or Five?*

[Once again Frank, even the tiniest bit of information would be helpful.]

I'm going to describe five golfers to you, the Ones, Twos, Threes, Fours and Fives.

ONES

Ones are rank beginners. To the One, a golf club is a foreign object and the ball is the enemy. Ones are learning how to hold the club, where to stand in relation to the ball and how to swing the club. Obviously (and mercifully for all concerned) they have never actually been on a golf course. Their number one thought is whether they will make contact with the ball. They worry about not embarrassing themselves.

TWOS

Twos often make contact with the ball. They have played the course and their handicaps range upwards from a starting point of about 24. Twos rarely if ever have broken 100 and their number one thought is trying to break 100. Golfers in this group who are newer to the game usually have *no one part* of their game that shows any effective consistency. More experienced golfers in this group have learned through compensation and trial and error to find various shots that sometimes work.

THREES

Threes make up the largest group of golfers. Their handicaps are about 23-13. They still duff some shots, but usually, at least one aspect of their game is working on any given day. Threes struggle to break 80 or 90, and, rarely and occasionally break 100 on the wrong side. Threes usually have at least one aspect of their game in which they are reasonably confident. Their number one thought is: when will I get IT all together on the same day.

FOURS

Fours have handicaps ranging from 12 and down to just short of being a pro. They golf consistently in the low to mid-80's and lower. The club champions are in this group. Although *they* are not happy with their games, their games are consistent enough to launch a One, Two or Three into golfing heaven. The thought of whether they will make contact with the ball never enters their minds. They may duff a few shots each season.

FIVES

Fives are the professional golfers, from the golf club professionals, to the touring pros.

WHAT

ARE

YOU?[3]

---

[3]   Once again, I urge you to figure out how you would rate
        yourself, and circle the appropriate flag. As you read on, you
        will find this exercise enlightening.

26

HOW THICK IS A THOUGHT?

"The Three thinks he's a Three and the Four thinks she's a Four."

---

o Juan, what type of golfer are you, a One, Two, Three, Four or Five?

[I guess I'm between a Three and a Four.]

How are you going to get to be a Four?

[I was hoping that you might tell me this.]

You've played with better golfers at your club, golfers that you would call a Four. What's the difference between a Three and a Four?

[I wish I knew.]

The answer is very simple.

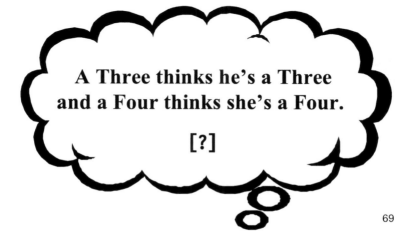

A Three thinks he's a Three and a Four thinks she's a Four.

[?]

I want you to picture all of the golfers in the world stacked one on top of the other according to their ability; first Ones, then Twos, etc. Now picture two golfers, a Three and a Four, right on the dividing line between Threes and Fours. You can see how close they are in ability and that the dividing line is very thin. *After all, how thick is a thought?*

The only difference between these two golfers is that the Three thinks he's a Three and the Four thinks she's a Four.

To the Three, this dividing line between the Land of Three and the Land of Four is an impermeable ceiling, which he thinks will hurt his head when he bumps it in his moments of golfing excellence. He is afraid to succeed for this reason and will not give himself permission to succeed. He has a built-in failure mechanism that prevents him from rising up to the Land of Four.

The Four (who once lived in the Land of Three) on the other hand, has dissolved this barrier, merely by "looking up". She has given herself permission to improve and succeed merely by thinking that she belongs there.

The Three thinks he's a Three and the Four thinks she's a Four.

27

WAYS YOU CAN
VS.
REASONS WHY YOU CAN'T

"In order to perform to the maximum of your potential, you must believe that you can do it. The way the human machine works is that the best you can perform is to the level of your expectations but no better."

Y ou've seen many golfers who don't seem to have great swings, score well. The difference between a 13 and a 9 handicap is only 4 shots on average per round. That's not really that much when you think about it. *So, why can't you be one level higher?*

[Well, I'm not a long hitter. My mid-to-long iron play is weak. I can never get all of my game working at the same time. The golf season in Toronto is so short that it takes time to get back my old form and then it seems the season is over.]

I bet that you just came up with 10 reasons why you can't play at a higher level.

[Four actually.]

This just proves my point that you can't get to the next level if you don't see yourself at that level. You're too caught up in why you *can't* get to the next level, rather than thinking about how you *can* get to the next level. You believe that your current ability level *limits* the scores that you can achieve. You will never get to the next level if you continue to think that you are a Three.

Every golfer has a *range of ability of performance* from poor to exceptional. In order to perform to the maximum of your potential, you must believe that you can do it. The way the *human machine* works is that the best you can perform is to the level of your expectations, but no better. Subconsciously, you will actually *resist* any action that will lead to inconsistency between your expectations and your performance. In other words, if you think of yourself as a Three, when you perform as a Three, you're happy that you have achieved your goal and you don't want to improve past maintaining that Three-ness.

Maybe the difference between the Three and the Four is the *confidence* the Four has to *go for every* putt and the belief that she can make it, as opposed to the Three's *cautious willingness to settle for* a two putt.

It's impossible to perform at a higher level than your own expectations.
You can't help it. You are a human being.

WHO IS THE BEST PUTTER IN THE WORLD?

"You are. Get IT?"

---

ho is the best putter in the world?

[Ben Crenshaw?]

No.

You are.

Get IT?

PLAYING
VS.
PRACTICING

ARE YOU PLAYING OR PRACTICING?

*"You can work on your game, but you don't
work the game of golf, you play IT. You have to
decide if you are working on your game or
playing the game."*

Juan, how long have you been practicing law?

[16 years.]

That's a lot of practicing. When are you going to start doing it
for real?

[Ha, ha.]

The same thing can be said for golf. One reason why some
golfers get frustrated, confused and disappointed is that they
think they are *playing* golf, when they are really *practicing* their
skills.

Playing golf is taking every shot with the club that gives you the
best probability of getting the ball into the hole in the fewest
number of strokes. I bet that 95 percent of the golf rounds that
are played are "practice" rounds where the players are trying this
or that, *rather than playing the game of golf.* In these "practice'
rounds, you see players hitting drivers every par four and par
five even though they can't keep the ball in the fairway.
If they haven't lost their ball, they're lucky if they
can chip it back on the
fairway.

76

Think how much farther ahead they would be if they had taken out the club in which they had the *most* confidence, rather than the club in which they had the *least* confidence.

Both playing golf and practicing golf are important, but you can only do one at a time. You must be crystal clear about which one you are doing at any given moment and measure your results accordingly.

Golf is a game. You can work on *your* game, but you don't work *the* game of golf, you play IT. You have to decide if you are working on *your* game or playing *the* game. As long as you understand which one you are doing, then you won't be confused or disappointed.

There's a place and a time to work on your game. You can even work on your game on the course. In fact, I encourage you to do this. Once you've made up your mind that you are playing a practice round, play a practice round. Keep a few extra balls in your pocket and play three or four shots from the same spot, especially from those places on the course that seem to give you trouble. Play different types of shots from a trouble spot, in search of one that works best for you.

But, when it's time to PLAY golf, PLAY golf.

THE QUESTION IS THE ANSWER

"Where is it that I want the ball to go and what club am I going to use?"

Pay attention to the questions that you ask yourself as an indicator of whether you are playing golf or practicing your game. There are only two questions when you are playing golf:

Where is it that I want the ball to go?

What club *am* I going to use?

"Where" and "what" are the questions that you ask when you are *playing* golf.

"How" and "why" are the questions that you ask when you are *practicing* your game.

31

PRACTICE PURPOSEFULLY
AND EXCELLENTLY

*"The purpose of practicing golf is so that you
will become more skillful and proficient on the
golf course. You are rehearsing for your
performance."*

---

ook up the word "practice" in the dictionary.

[I know what the word "practice" means.]

I know that you don't want to do this, but do it anyway.

[Okay *"repeated performance or systematic exercise
for the purpose of acquiring skill or proficiency"*.]

If you practice a musical instrument, you do it so that you will
be able to perform in a recital or a concert. You *rehearse* for
your *performance*. The purpose of practicing golf is so that you
will become more skillful and proficient on the golf course.

You are also rehearsing
for your performance. The
purpose of the driving
range is *not* simply to
stand there and whack out
a bucket of balls. Most
people I see spend their
time on the range
practicing their mistakes
over and over again. No
wonder they get so
proficient at their

mistakes.   It's funny to imagine a violinist rehearsing for a concert the way that most golfers practice golf on the driving range.

> *Practice golf so that your body and your mind*
> *will play the same tune every day.*

Therefore, practice on the range *exactly* like you would play on the course.

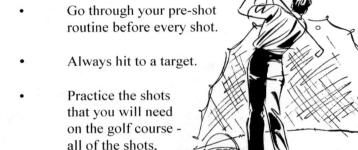

•   Go through your pre-shot routine before every shot.

•   Always hit to a target.

•   Practice the shots that you will need on the golf course - all of the shots, including chipping out from the trees.

•   Play an imaginary 18-hole round of golf on the driving range exactly as you would play on the course, including changing your club from shot to shot.

Work on your GAME, which is not just practicing the golf swing, but practicing the game of golf. Practice the shot, not the swing.

If you want to perform as a winner,
then practice like a winner.

Practice purposefully and excellently.

32

PH. D (WEDGE)

"If you are a deadly wedge player, then you won't even need your putter."

When we first met, you had just graduated from law school. You gave me one of your business cards which said "Jonathan H. Fine, B.Sc., LL.B." I guess to be a lawyer, you needed a degree in B.S. first.

[You're not really that funny, you know.]

In golf, there is an *unofficial* degree that you can earn. It's called *Ph. D (wedge)*. If you earn this degree, you have the right to call yourself Dr. Wedge.

How important is your wedge play? Most people say that your putter is the most important club. I disagree. I think your wedges are your most important clubs. If you are a deadly wedge player, then you won't even need your putter.

[How much should I practice wedges?]

When you toss a ball onto the green, you instinctively know where to toss the ball and what trajectory to use to get the ball to your target. Practice your wedges until you believe that you have the same proficiency. Concentrate on direction and sinking every chip.

You are lucky because you belong to a golf club where you can go out on the course early in the mornings or late at night and practice by yourself. There's no substitute for practicing almost the exact shots that you will have to make tomorrow or the next day. Fill your pockets with golf balls and practice these shots from about 50-60 yards in, moving forward 5 yards at a time. Notice how much you choke down on the club; whether you take a full back swing or something less; how far your ball comes to rest from its mark on the green.

Put 10 balls in a bunker and see if you can get them all within a 3-foot circle of the hole. And Juan, always remember to fill in your divots, repair your ball marks on the green and rake the bunkers.

Practice your wedges until your friends call you Dr. Wedge.

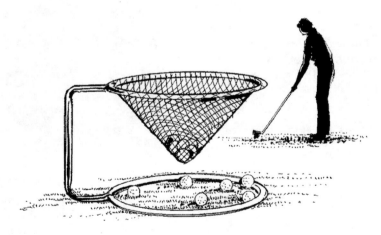

And then practice them some more.

33

FG1, G1, FG2, G2, FS1

"See if you can play a round with only FG1, G1, FG2, G2 or FS1s on your scorecard."

Some people will give you a page-long list of statistics that you can keep track of every round. I disagree with this for many reasons but the two most important are that it's too distracting and it's unnecessary. Aside from your score, it is helpful however, to keep track of:

- fairways hit (even if it's in the rough, if you are able to make your shot, count it as a fairway hit and mark an "F").

- greens in regulation (if you are putting, even if it's on the fringe, count it as a green hit and mark a "G").

- number of putts.

- bunker shots (mark an "S").

As you mark your score, record the results. Circle your pars and birdies and add ** to your birdies. See if you can play a round with only FG1, G1, FG2, G2 or FS1s on your scorecard.

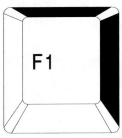

[What about GOs and FGOs? Those would be eagles. Don't you want to see those?]

Eagles are good scores, obviously, but you will see that you will get more satisfaction from a "circle-F1", meaning that you saved par after hitting the fairway but not the green. That's playing the game of golf.

SIX PARS IS AN 84

"You can break 80 if you get just five more pars."

I remember when you won a tournament match once and you shot 84 and it was one of your best scores. After the match I asked you how many pars you had made, and you told me six. You couldn't believe that you only had six pars, but think about it. On a par 72 course, if you get only six pars, you score an 84 if you bogey the rest of the holes. Six pars - that's all it takes to shoot 84.

Now stop for a moment and think how close you are to 80 and to breaking 80. You can break 80 if you get just five more pars.

Keep track of the total number of pars that you make each round and the average number of pars that you make over the course of a season. I think you will find it interesting.

THE FIVE HARDEST SHOTS

*"All of your shots are important, but it is how
you perform on these shots that will usually tell
the story of your round."*

I n any round of golf, there are about two dozen critical
shots, in which excellent execution is critical. Don't get
me wrong, all of your shots are important, but it is how
you perform on these shots that will usually tell the
story of your round. Among these two dozen shots, I'll bet there
are at least five that most golfers find the *most difficult* on their
course. Think about your course. *Do you know which five shots
I'm talking about?*

Why not figure out which these shots
are for you, and then go out on your
course early one morning or late one
evening and practice these five shots.
Apparently, the way that you are
playing them is not right for you, so
try to find *alternative ways to play
the hole. Open your mind* to all of
the different ways. Think of the most
unconventional way to play the
shot and then see what
happens. You'll be
surprised. Find the
safest way for you
to get the ball into
the hole in the fewest number
of strokes. I bet that you can save yourself three
to five strokes a round.

PLAY THE LADIES' TEES

*"Playing golf from the ladies' tees is like
making love to a new woman."*

 Juan, I want you to play a game from the ladies' tees.

[Frank, some days I have a hard enough time getting a game.]

I know that you are probably saying that you would be embarrassed to do this.

[No kidding.]

Why? All you are doing is giving yourself the opportunity of playing your course from a new perspective. You'll have to rethink every shot, use different clubs and make much different decisions than you are used to making. Playing golf from the ladies' tees is like making love to a new woman. Try it, I think you might like it.

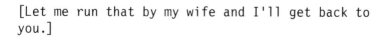

[Let me run that by my wife and I'll get back to you.]

PLAY A COMPLETELY DIFFERENT GAME

"The act of 'trying' creates tension and anxiety, and distracts your attention from your goal of getting the ball into the hole in the fewest number of strokes."

Every golfer goes through hot and cold cycles. Often, when our "A" game deserts us, the pressure builds and *we try harder* to get back to our old selves. *Trying harder doesn't work.* In fact, it usually just makes things worse because the act of "trying" creates tension and anxiety, and distracts your attention from your goal of getting the ball into the hole in the fewest number of strokes. When you find that you are trying too hard, do something completely different.

[Like ...?]

Play a completely different game. Use different clubs than you would normally use. Tee-off with an iron or a 5-wood instead of your driver. If you usually play a 3-wood as your second shot, to get you within range of your lob wedge, hit two mid-irons instead.

Make a conscious effort to play a completely different game and see what happens.

38

MENTAL PRACTICE: YOUR BRAIN IS A MUSCLE, EXERCISE IT.

"In a close competition, the winning difference can be one thought, yet who ever practices the most important part of the game. Most golfers spend 100 percent of their time practicing 5 to 10 percent of the game. I don't get it!"

G olf is 90 percent, even 95 percent mental. In a close competition, the winning difference can be one thought, yet who ever *practices* the most important part of the game. Most golfers spend 100 percent of their time practicing 5 to 10 percent of the game. I don't get it! If you really want to improve, if you are really committed to improving, then you've got to exercise your brain. Exercising your brain is really *reprogramming your brain for golfing success.* Think of your brain as a muscle and exercise it. In fact, mental exercise is something that you can do anywhere.

[Sort of like winter daydreaming about golf.]

89

Here are some things that you can do to exercise your brain:

• After each round, go through your score card and replay your good shots in your mind, even if there's only one.

• After a bad shot, imagine the way you wanted it to turn out.

• Remember your successes and relive them just as if you were playing them.

• Play the course in your mind.

• Think about a putt dropping over and over and over again. Hear the sound. Feel the excitement.

• Stare at a golf ball for 5 minutes a day. Personify it. Make friends with it. Imagine what it is like to be a golf ball. How do its dimples affect its flight? How does it feel when it is struck perfectly?

**GETTING THE BALL
INTO THE HOLE
IN THE FEWEST
NUMBER OF STROKES**

HOW CAN I GET THE BALL INTO THE HOLE IN THE FEWEST NUMBER OF STROKES?

"If you are thinking about anything other than how to get the ball into the hole in the fewest number of strokes, then you are not playing the game of golf."

G olf really is a very simple game. Too often we forget that IT is both *simple,* and a *game. Get the ball into the hole in the fewest number of strokes.* Can you think of a simpler game? Even baseball is more complicated. As you stand over your ball, are *you* thinking about how you can get the ball into the hole in the fewest number of strokes, or are you thinking about something else?

[First, I've got to get the correct grip, and then I've got to remember to stand tall, be proud like a matador, and then to start my back swing ...]

Enough! You've proved my point. For most of us, getting the ball into the hole in the fewest number of strokes is the farthest thing from our minds. Whether it is merely making sure that you don't whiff, or thinking about the angle of your swing plane, if you are thinking about *anything* other than how to get the ball into the hole in the fewest number of strokes, then you are not *playing* the *game* of golf.

[That would surprise a few million people on this planet.   What have we been playing if not the game of golf?]

You've been playing the game of "golf swing".   That's what *you* are thinking about when you are addressing the ball. Don't get me wrong. There's nothing wrong with practicing your golf swing, but don't confuse practicing "the golf swing" with "playing golf". Sometimes I think that golfers need the golfing equivalent of baseball's umpire to announce "play ball" to remind us that the *game* has begun and that "batting practice" is over.

[But, I have to work on my swing.]

Great, but sooner or later it's going to be time to *play golf.* And when it's time to play golf, PLAY GOLF! Forget about fixing. *You've got to play with what you've got.*

Remember that golf is a game of accuracy, not strength. Golf is a game of score, not distance. Why do you insist on taking out the Big Dog again, when all the Big Dog wants to do is the Big Slice into the woods?

[Well, some days the Big Dog isn't working.]

If the Big Dog doesn't want to work for you, let him sleep for the day. Play golf. If you were driving your car and it kept veering to the left and crashing into the guard rail, what would you do?

Let me put it another way. If you want to shoot the best scores
that *you* can possibly shoot, then only one thing matters: getting
the ball into the hole in the fewest number of strokes. Once you
focus on this simple thought, *you give yourself permission* to
accept your swing, however good or bad it is that day, and get
down to the business of playing golf. Once you do this, every
decision that you make will be based upon one thought:

How can I get the ball
into the hole
in the fewest number of strokes?

USE ONE MORE CLUB

*"Most of the time, if you had used one more
club, you probably would have been closer to
the hole"*

---

 re you usually short or long?

[In what respect, Frank?]

I bet that most of the time, your approach shots to the green are
short of the flagstick. Sometimes, there's good reason to be
short of the flagstick, but most of the time, if you had used one
more club, you probably would have
been closer to the hole.

Unless there is trouble at the back of the green,
use one more club and see what happens.

41

PUTTING:
YOUR *COUP DE GRACE*

"Low scores just don't happen, they are made ... putting is where you can slash your scores and destroy your opponents."

I remember you telling me a story about how you were cross-examining a witness and you asked him whether your client had coerced him by physical force. *Do you remember the witness's answer?*

[How could I forget. He said *"not by physical force, but by mental force!"*.]

Low scores just don't happen, they are made. Have you ever noticed that quite often a low handicap player will miss the green, just like you, but he or she walks away with a par, and you with a bogey or worse? Even if you make what you think is a great chip, remember that *it's not a great chip unless you make the putt.* Putting is where you can slash your scores and destroy your opponents. Putting is your *coup de grace.*

How would a matador putt? Be bold on the putting green. Expect to make every putt. Want IT so much that you can feel your mind guiding the ball into the hole. *Use mental force.*

Summon the forces of the universe

to direct the ball
into the hole.

IF IT'S YOUR DAY, THE PUTTS WILL DROP

"It's almost as if it's not you putting but an energy force surrounding your body that takes over and makes the putts."

———————————

"**G**olf", should be called "putting" because good scores and golf matches are decided on the greens. Putting is the name of the game. Whether it's a 40-foot snake, or consistently dropping 6-footers, good putting has a debilitating effect on an opponent.

There are those days when your putts seem to be drawn toward and into the hole. It's almost as if it's not *you* putting, *but an energy force surrounding your body that takes over* and makes the putts. Sometimes you don't realize IT until after the round, but if early in the round the putts are dropping, *recognize that it's your day.* Anything you touch is going to go in, or at least be within a tap in. Knowing this, you can stand up to your putts with the highest confidence, knowing that your invisible putting friend will take over.

Savor these days.
They're YOUR days.
Your putts WILL d
  r
   o
    p.

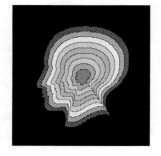

THIS IS A PUTT
I MAKE ALL OF THE TIME

*"How many times do you think Babe Ruth
pointed to right field and then promptly popped
out?"*

H *ow great would it be if just before you putt, you
announce to your playing partners: "This is a putt I
make all of the time," and
then you sink it?*

[They'd be talking to
themselves for two holes.]

Not only that, but
you'd be well on your
way to becoming *a
legend in your own
mind*, which is exactly
what you want.

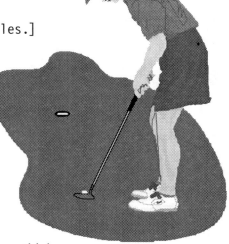

[But what if I don't
sink the putt, they'd
think I am a jerk?]

Juan, how many times do you think
Babe Ruth pointed to right field *and then promptly popped out?*

EVERY PUTT IS MAKEABLE IN MANY DIFFERENT WAYS

"On a green, 6 inches is like a highway."

T he hole is 4.25 inches in diameter while a ball is just over 1.5 inches in diameter. According to my calculations, assuming that a ball that is at least half-way over the edge of the cup will fall in, there's a pathway of about 6 inches leading to the hole. *On a green, 6 inches is like a highway.* On the practice green, use a string and some tees to mark out that highway. During your round, survey each putt and find that six-inch corridor and then putt the ball into the hole.

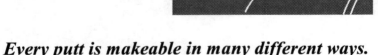

Every putt is makeable in many different ways.

45

ADVICE ON
GETTING OUT OF THE WOODS

"Make sure you get out."

---

ake sure you get out.

You only need one great shot per hole.[1]

This isn't going to be it!

---

[1] See Chapter 17 of *Golf Is a Very Simple Game*.

46

NERVOUS ON THE FIRST TEE

*"Focus on your target. That's how you deal
with your nerves on the first tee."*

I remember you were playing in a best ball match with your friend Brian as your partner. You were nervous because there was a crowd and you really wanted to begin the match with a good shot, especially in front of all those people. As you stood on the first tee, I could see that you were *thinking about your nervousness*, rather than *where* you wanted your first shot to go.

Focus on your target. *That's how you deal with your nerves on the first tee.* Do you remember where your drive went?

[Long straight and in the middle of the fairway?]

Good news and bad news, Juan. Your ball landed right in the middle of the flower bed, but fortunately for you, just *past* the ladies' tees!

Golf is a very simple game. Get the ball into the hole in the fewest number of strokes. If you are thinking about anything other than getting the ball into the hole in the fewest number of strokes then you should be nervous, because you are setting yourself up for failure.

IF YOU ARE GOING TO PLAY SAFE, PLAY SAFE!

"Keep the ball in play, again"

---

*H**ow many times have you tried to lay up short of the river on your ninth hole, only to hit the ball into the river?*

[I give up, how many?]

Makes you feel really stupid, doesn't it, Juan? Well, there's good reason for that! How many times have I told you? *If you are going to play safe, play safe!*

When you are playing safe and laying up, choose the club that you feel will leave you *absolutely* safe even if you really click it. In other words, if you are unsure what club to hit, choose the higher lofted club. Often times, when we lay up, we hit our best shots because we take an easy swing, making full and sharp impact with the ball because we are relaxed. As well, remember to take into account hills, sloping banks and variations in the composition of fairways, all of which can result in unwanted distance or errant direction. An iron into a soft green lands differently than the same shot landing on a firm, sloping fairway. Judge your distances accordingly, taking the unexpected into consideration.

Keep the ball in play, again.

48

BRING IT
TO A GRINDING HALT

*"A golf swing is a process not an event that
begins with the pre-shot routine and ends with
you watching your ball fly through the air."*

H *ow many times have you started your back swing,
only to realize that something just didn't feel right?*

There's definitely a point of no return, which before
you reach, you can cause yourself to stop your swing. You
know that only on rare occasions when you get this
feeling do you hit a good shot, so why don't you just
bring your swing to a grinding halt?

One reason is because you may be
having a poor round and
you just don't care.
Another reason is
because your
concentration isn't sharp
and you have reached the
point of no return
before you realize
that you have that
uncomfortable feeling.

If you *do* happen to have the courage, confidence and presence
of mind to bring your swing to a grinding halt, start your pre-
swing routine all over again. Don't let the demons convince you
that because you did it before to your first attempt, you don't

have to do it again. That's just an excuse. That's an exception
to the rule. That's a formula for failure. A golf swing is a
process not an event that begins with the pre-shot routine and
ends with you watching your ball fly through the air.

Sometimes, as you are standing over your ball,
something happens and you lose your
perspective and alignment relative to your
target. When you feel this, *how can you get
your proper perspective back?* By looking at
your target while you are still in your address
position with your head bent down and
sideways, or, by standing straight and tall
looking forward to your target?

[I think I'll take door number
two.]

49

THE PRE-SHOT ROUTINE

"Repetition and consistency is the key to success."

Good golfers are disciplined because they know that *repetition and consistency* is the key to success. Consistent shot-making begins long before you take your swing. You must develop a routine, which begins for the *next* shot as soon as you have completed your *last* shot, and ends with you following your ball as it sails toward its eventual resting place. Your pre-shot routine commences with you reminding yourself that golf is played one shot at a time, that the last shot is now finished and that *the only thing that matters now is the next shot.*

As you are approaching your ball, you are considering all of the different factors that might influence your club selection and the type of shot that you will take. As you get nearer to your ball, start thinking about your target and as you walk to your ball, position yourself so that your ball and the target are directly in front of you. This will burn the target and the intended line of flight into your mind and help you with your alignment.

107

Now here's the really important part. Once you have decided what club to use, take your practice swing away from the ball. Once you have reminded your body of the swing, then once again, stand behind the ball, focus on your target and get your alignment and bearings. Sometimes it helps to visualize a huge sheet of glass extending from your target through your ball and extending past you. If you have that in your mind, then all you have to do to get the correct alignment is to line up your shoulders, knees and hips parallel to that plane.

The reason why I tell you to take your practice swing away from the ball rather than once you have addressed the ball is because the last thing that you want to think about before you hit the ball is the target. If you choose your target and *then* focus on the mechanics of the swing, you run the risk of forgetting your target. The images of the target in your mind will fade away like the way the light of a LED gradually, but quickly dissipates.

YOUR LOVER
OR A TEMPTRESS?

"Know the difference between the voice of your lover, and that of a temptress."

T here are some holes that cry out for you to go for IT. These are the holes that don't penalize you for an errant shot - holes with wide fairways and no out of bounds. On these holes, if and only if you are feeling good, *let `im go.* Other holes tempt and tease you but mete out severe consequences for failure.

Know the difference between the voice of your lover, and that of a temptress.

When a hole cries out for you to go for IT, go for IT.

When a hole entices you with rewards only if you risk everything, take a cold shower!

MAINTAINING
YOUR
COMMITMENT

HOW ARE YOU GOING TO MAINTAIN YOUR COMMITMENT REGARDLESS OF WHATEVER HAPPENS ON THE GOLF COURSE?

"This is a question of discipline, attitude and belief. A question of psyching up, getting into and staying in The Zone. Capturing IT."

---

*H*ow are you going to maintain your commitment regardless of whatever happens on the golf course?

This is a question of discipline, attitude and belief. A question of psyching up, getting into and *staying in* The Zone. Capturing IT. Maintaining your focus for 18 holes of golf.

Do you have a *solid strategy* that you will rely on to keep yourself from getting upset, frustrated or panicky throughout a round of golf? Or, are you just going to drive the ball aimlessly and see where you end up?

What image better describes the clarity and organization of your mental strategy:

A swarm of flies or a formation of Canadian geese?

HEAD
IN THE RIGHT DIRECTION

"You forgot the most important part of your equipment."

J uan, pretend that you are getting everything together that you'll need for a round of golf. List everything that you'll need.

[Bag, clubs, balls, shoes, gloves, hat, tees, ball markers, green repair tool, rain gear, umbrella, sunscreen. I guess that's it.]

You forgot the most important part of your equipment.

[What?]

Your head!

A JOURNEY OF 1,000 MILES
STARTS WITH A SINGLE STEP

*"What is it that stands in the way of achieving
maximum possible potential?"*

---

 *id you ever hear the ancient Chinese proverb: "a
journey of a thousand miles starts with a single
step?"*

[I think I may have gotten it in a fortune cookie
once, but other than that ...]

A round of golf is a journey of 18 holes that starts with a single
shot. *Why is it that we can't make
that journey playing the best golf
that we can possibly play? What
stands in the way?*

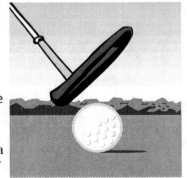

[Well, I would think that
skill and ability might have
something to do with it.]

A person's skill and ability is not a
fixed point, but rather a range. Of
all the sports that I can think of,
this is probably most evident in golf. Everyone has four basic
levels of performance: poor, average, peak and maximum
possible potential. *What is it that stands in the way of achieving
maximum possible potential?*

[Does it have anything to do with how we program our
minds?]

54

BE GOOD = FEEL GOOD = THINK GOOD = FEEL GOOD = BE GOOD

"Try IT. IT really works. And IT will work for you, if you believe that IT will work for you."

*O*n those days when you play your best golf, how do you feel? Are you happy and cheerful?[1] I trust that your answer is "yes", and assuming that to be the case, I trust you will agree with me that playing good golf makes you feel good.

[Duh!]

Think about those days when you are playing good. What are you thinking about? Are you thinking about how lousy life is? Are you thinking, *"today is the worst day of my life and I am a terrible golfer"?* I don't think so! When you play good golf, you feel good and you are thinking good thoughts.

---

[1] [Delighted, delightful, elated, ecstatic, excited, exhilarated, gleeful, invigorated, jubilant, lively, merry, optimistic, perky, pleased, radiant, rollicking, spirited, sunny ... Okay, so I used the thesaurus. What's the big deal?]

Playing good, feeling good and thinking good are part of an equation. Playing good golf makes you feel good and think good. Thinking good thoughts makes you feel good. If you feel good, then you will have confidence in yourself and in your game, which in turn gives you the best opportunity to play well and shoot a good score.

Be Good = Feel Good = Think Good

The question is: *how can you get yourself feeling good before and throughout every round?* If you can do this then you give yourself the opportunity to play better than you ever imagined; *better than you ever believed you could play.*

The answer is so simple and easy to do.

Choose to think good thoughts.

Think Good = Feel Good = Be Good

WHAT IF you can improve your golf just by thinking differently?

WHAT IF you can increase the level of your performance by thinking the same thoughts that make The Needle spin faster?

WHAT IF by merely thinking happy thoughts, you can repel negativity?

WHAT IF other people will be attracted to you, just because of what you are thinking?

WHAT IF you can create a happy world around you, just by thinking happy thoughts?

Try IT. IT really works.

***And IT WILL work for you,
if you believe that IT will work for you.***

55

USING THE NEEDLE

"You have a choice, and it's that decision that programs your mind."

---

*D*o you want to know how you can get yourself feeling good before and throughout every round?

[Yes]

If your brain is a fleshy computer, then you can program or train your mind to think only good thoughts. You can *choose to remember* only the good things that happen to you. Are you going to remember the one great shot or the three not so great shots?

[Choose to remember?]

Yes, choose. You have a choice, *and it's that decision that programs your mind.* It's that choice that determines how you perceive yourself as a golfer. *You are in total control of your thoughts and your actions.* That's a scary thought isn't it. *Choose feeling good and you will feel good.* Sounds too simple? IT is simple and IT's true, if you believe IT to be true! In fact, you as a human being have the ability to turn your feelings of happiness up and down in the same way you can dim or brighten the lights in your dining room!

IT is simple and IT's true, if you believe IT to be true!

Try this experiment. Sit down. Take a deep breath and let it out. Think about the most incredibly amazing thing that could ever happen to you. Something that makes your spine tingle. What is it? The thought that made *The Needle* spin like a helicopter. Tell me.

[It's playing Johnny B. Goode in front of 100,000 people at an outdoor summer rock concert.]

Notice how you feel. Are you smiling? Do you feel energized? Are you happy? Can you feel your personal light brighten? Now, think about the worst, most awful, disgusting, depressing thing that could ever happen to you. How do you feel? Are you weak? Do you feel flat and depressed? Now, capture that amazing good feeling again. Concentrate on IT until you feel your light shining bright. If you have done this with an open mind, believing that IT will work, you will see that you can turn on and off, dim and brighten your "light" at will. Can you see how this *might* help you during a round of golf?

[It's funny that you say that because on the way to the club, I often drive with my favorite music blaring, imaging myself singing to a huge crowd. By the time I get to the club, I am really feeling good.]

That's good. You are revving up your energy engine, getting yourself in the best frame of mind and spirit to ride the 18-hole emotional roller coaster.

VRRRRRMM
VRRRRRMM

56

WORDS AND IDEAS CAN BE BARRIERS AND PRISONS: WHAT'S YOUR HANDICAP?

"Imagine if you didn't know that you were a 15-handicap, but just a golfer...Calling a par-four, a par-four, instead of simply "the second hole", suggests to the golfer that taking four strokes is the objective."

W ords and ideas can act as walls and bullets, stopping us dead in our tracks, preventing us from taking action and worse yet, from living our dreams. Words and ideas *give definition* to our lives by forming a metaphorical shell around us, which not only comforts and protects us, but also *imprisons us*.

[Do you mean that we are restricted in our thinking by the very words and ideas that we use to define the boundaries of our awareness?]

Words and ideas *can be* walls and bullets to *some* golfers, stopping them dead in their tracks on the road to improvement. Words and ideas are *not* walls and bullets to a golfer who is *committed* to playing the best golf that he or she can possibly play. Words and ideas are *not* walls and bullets to a golfer who believes that it is possible to *always* play the best golf that he or she can possibly play.

Commitment, belief and an open mind are the mental tools that break the shell. Commitment, belief and an open mind remove the barriers and give you both the permission and impetus that you need to excel day after day after day.

Somebody tol' me that *"your handicap is your handicap."* In other words, a golfer's handicap is an idea that can limit performance. For example, if you ask someone how he golfs, he will likely tell you his handicap as if it was a static piece of information.

Stating your handicap, for most golfers, is almost an admission that you aren't going to be getting any better.

Imagine if you didn't know that you were a 15-handicap, but just a golfer. Putting the label of a 15-handicap on someone is a barrier which keeps them trapped. Calling a par-four, a par-four, instead of simply "the second hole", suggests to the golfer that taking four strokes is the objective. I thought the objective was to get the ball into the hole in the fewest number of strokes.

You can always improve.
Give yourself a chance to do so
by REFUSING
to define and limit your golfing ability
by your current handicap.

57

FEAR AND HOPE
ARE THE SAME THING

"Your brain doesn't care what you think about, makes no judgments about your thoughts and can't distinguish positive from negative thoughts."

---

*I*f I told you that Fear and Hope were the same thing, what would you say?

[I'd say that you're the type of person who looks forward to being afraid.]

Fear is your belief about what could or might happen in the future. And you act accordingly.

[You could say that Hope is your belief about what could or might happen in the future.]

Exactly! And you act accordingly.

Hope and Fear are exactly the same thing; beliefs about to what might or could happen in the future. The *difference* between the two is determined by how your brain is programmed to interpret what you think about. Visualization, goal-setting, positive self-talk, etc., are all

122

simply brain-programming tools to assist you in focusing on and achieving your *desired* beliefs about what might or could happen in the future.

[But you just said that Hope and Fear were exactly the same. How can there be a difference between them?]

Your brain doesn't care what you think about, makes no judgments about your thoughts and can't distinguish positive from negative thoughts. On one level, your brain's function is to co-ordinate your actions with your thoughts. If you think about things that make *The Needle* grind to a halt, then your brain will oblige and design your very own personalized perfect life consumed and driven by Fear.

On the other hand, if your thoughts can make *The Needle* spin like a helicopter, your life will be defined by Hope and Happiness.

58

HELICOPTER WORDS

T he words that YOUR brain uses define how YOU experience YOUR life.

The following brain-words typify the thoughts of someone who can make *The Needle* spin like a helicopter:

wonderment, curiosity, interest, amazement, awe, joy, exhilaration, elation, thrill, stimulation, motivation, drive, ambition, affection, friendliness, calmness, passion, vigor, vitality, vivacity, vibrance, power, strength, stamina, eagerness, devotion, intensity, prominence, majesty, greatness, exceptional, cherished, scrupulous, honorable, worthy, distinct, quality, elite, select, desire, intuition, insight, vision, imagination, accomplishment, dreams, hope, zeal, energy, inspiration, excitement, fun, delight, results, breakthrough, discovery, innovation, freedom, liberated, emancipated, absolute, spark, influence, possibility, ease, boldness, independence, individuality, authentic, originality, creativity, brilliance, mastery, ingenuity, resourcefulness, confidence, admiration, optimism, respect, reverence, honor, happiness, composure, serenity, control, spunk, endurance, life, essence, spirit, animation, gusto, pep, cheer, joviality, potency, command, capable, ability, potential, promise, skill, courageous, effectiveness, concentration, flair, panache, interesting, charisma, magnificence, acumen, style, class, élan, grace, balance, aptitude, talent, marvel, resilience, love, appreciative, understanding, dedication, distinguished, eminence, prominent, heroic, outstanding, superb, monumental, important, phenomenal, unique, ethical, honest, upstanding, decent, fair, right, dependable, solid, reliable, accountable, responsible, faithful, distinctive, special, knowledgeable, experienced, seasoned, wise, achievement, success, proficiency, belief, faith, trust, ambition, opportunity, luck, chance, charm, magic, impetus, catalyst, revelation, encouragement, entertaining, merry, lively, amusing, sport, laugh, frolic, play, rollicking, pleasure, game, joke, enchant, enthral, fascination, glorious, triumphant, enjoyable, unfettered, clear, candid, unconstrained, open, present, complete, positive, carte blanche, advance, augment, broaden, expand, increase, continue, poise, spontaneity, prosperity, comfort, self-sufficient, self-reliance, self-assurance, bona fide, natural, sincere, unaffected, radiance, resplendence, splendor, conviction, purpose, determination, integrity, moral, character, reputable, acclaimed, esteemed, gratified, satisfied, composed, humane, charitable, dignified, tolerant, cool, unruffled, daring, perseverance, persistence, tenacity, being, soul, alert, observant, interested, considerate, courteous, unprecented, classic, exceptional, imperial, valiant, dauntless, epic, legendary, extraordinary, sensational, spectacular, remarkable, gracious, conscientious, scrupulous, upstanding, principled, incorruptible, just pleasant, exemplary, good, righteous[1]

Which words describe your thoughts? = Which words describe your life? = Which words describe your thoughts on the golf course?

---

[1]   Doesn't that make you feel good?

59

NEEDLE STOPPING WORDS

T he words that YOUR brain uses define how YOU experience YOUR life.

The following words can make *YOUR NEEDLE* grind to a halt:

cynicism, fear, dread, anxiety, apathy, worry, consternation, apprehension, trepidation, pessimism, contempt, gloom, disdain, unhappiness, aversion, rejection, indifference, weakness, lethargy, animosity, disloyalty, betrayal, hostility, agitation, roughness, aggravation, nervousness, commotion, indifference, melancholy, infirmity, subservience, inability, fragility, loathing, hate, impatience, scorn, nonchalance, irreverence, mediocre, common, average, inconsequential, despise, unworthy, corrupt, disreputable, vague, harmful, blind, lost, failure, sad, defeat, ineptitude, despair, doubt, deterrent, discouragement, tumult, confusion, disturbance, agitation, painful, boredom, tedious, dull, disappointed, conventionality, dependency, slavery, bound, chained, restrained, handcuffed, blocked, reserved, confined, imprisoned, detached, disengaged, closed, suppressed, questionable, dubious, negative, insignificant, restricted, limited, withdraw, decrease, stop, depress,

127

extinguish, stifle, quell, lull, difficulty, stress, denial, self-indulgent, insincere, counterfeit, drab, trifle, immoral, treacherous, malice, selfishness, greedy, stingy, hysterical, rough, commotion, timid, ill, unstable, death, lifelessness, hesitant, disgrace, sorrow, harsh, coarse, despicable, lowly, terrible, inferior, typical, devious, unscrupulous, obscene, intolerable, rude, improper

Which words describe your thoughts? = Which words describe your life? = Which words describe your thoughts on the golf course?

60

MUDDLE YOUR WAY
AROUND THE COURSE

"I'm going to tell you the secret of life!"

We've talked about life many times and how it's like a journey. Well, perhaps the most important advice I ever learned was from a member at your club who was very successful at everything he did. One day I asked him, *"How do you do this. You're very popular with your friends. You've got a terrific family. You make a lot of money. Every deal that you go into seems to turn out good. You are the epitome of what our society calls a success. How do you do it? I want to know. I'd like to be a success like you."*

He said to me, *"Frank, come here. I'm going to tell you the secret of life!"*

I said ,*"Great, what is it?"*

He said, *"I just muddle my way through every day."*

I said, *"Come on, give me a break. You know, you have*

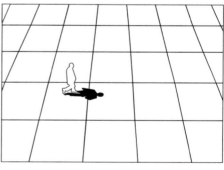

got to have a better grasp on where you're going than that."

He said, *"No, I just muddle my way through every day. I don't know what's going to happen. I can't predict the future. No one can. I just wake up, put my clothes on and I start walking. You think that I'm successful, but the truth is that I have lots of failures. I just succeed more than I fail."*

129

[What the heck does *this* have to do with *golf*?]

You figure IT out.

EXCELLENCE AND INTEGRITY

*"Golfing with excellence and integrity leaves
room for error and success."*

---

*A*lways let excellence and integrity be your goal, in life
and in golf.

Excellence means being remarkably good; excelling,
but not being perfect. *Integrity* means being sound, honest and
whole. If you live excellence and integrity you can sleep at
night.

Golf is a game determined by the quality of your bad shots.
Making perfection your goal in a game that is defined by error is
a one-way ticket in the wrong direction. One bad shot and you
have failed.

***Golfing with excellence and integrity
leaves room for error and success.***

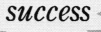

THOMAS EDISON
WAS A FAILURE
(UNTIL HE SUCCEEDED)

"In golf, you never know how your round is going to turn out. The best you can do is to muddle your way through the round from shot to shot, one shot at a time and enjoy IT."

homas Edison failed ten thousand times before he invented the lightbulb. Do you know what Thomas Edison said after he had failed 10,000 times?

[It's getting dark and now would be an excellent time for this damn thing to work.]

"Now I know ten thousand things that don't work."

[He just didn't care about failure.]

Do you think that Thomas Edison knew when he started, that he was going to invent the lightbulb?

[Yes.]

I don't think so! Thomas Edison, was just a guy who sat down and started doing some experiments, and happened to invent the lightbulb.

Similarly, in golf, *you never know how your round is going to turn out (even if you triple-bogey the first hole).* The best you can do is to muddle your way through the round from shot to shot, one shot at a time and enjoy IT. *That's golf.* That's the elusive, sultry, teasing thing that is the game of golf.

Accept IT.

Enjoy IT.

Embrace IT.

Love IT.

63

EVERY SHOT
IS AN OPPORTUNITY
FOR GREATNESS

"Look for and expect opportunity, and you will find IT. You won't even notice IT, if you're not looking for IT."

G olf, like life, is not about truth. *IT is about what we believe to be true.* Golf is a game of attitude and perception, not truth. Each person perceives events in his or her own way. There is an old story about a glass which has some water in it. *Is the glass half full or half empty?* On the days when your putts are not dropping, *do you tell yourself that you are a bad putter, or that you are a good putter, just having a bad day?* It's a matter of attitude and perception.

Our perception of events (in other words, how our brain processes information) and the judgments that we make, shape what we perceive as our experiences, actions, successes and failures. Take, for example, a shot that doesn't end up where you want it to go. Let's say it ends up in a bunker. How you perceive that shot will determine how you feel, how you play and what you think about your abilities as a golfer. Is it a *bad* shot? Is it *simply* a shot that didn't go where you wanted it to go? Is it one of your *typically* bad shots because you are a bad golfer? Is it *just one of many shots* that you will take today? *Is it an opportunity for greatness?*

[A shot that lands in the bunker is an opportunity
for greatness? I don't think so. I say it's more
like my punishment for hitting a poor approach shot.
And I'm not a very good sand player. Bottom line.
I just boarded the boat to double-bogeyland!]

Let me ask you a question. Have you ever holed out from a bunker, chipped in from just off the green or sunk a 40-foot putt?

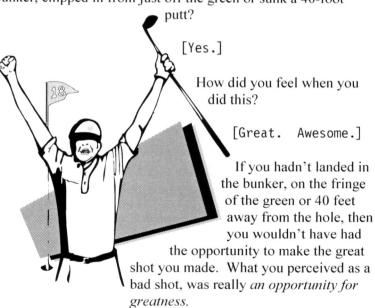

[Yes.]

How did you feel when you did this?

[Great. Awesome.]

If you hadn't landed in the bunker, on the fringe of the green or 40 feet away from the hole, then you wouldn't have had the opportunity to make the great shot you made. What you perceived as a bad shot, was really *an opportunity for greatness.*

Every shot is an opportunity for greatness!

Somebody once told me that *success is moving from failure to failure without loss of enthusiasm.* I guess when you think about it, this can describe golf. More importantly, however, it defines an attitude that is essential for winning and enjoyable golf.

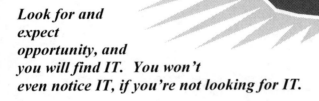

Look for and expect opportunity, and you will find IT. You won't even notice IT, if you're not looking for IT.

Golf is a game that is constantly giving us opportunities to achieve greatness.

64

YABBIT

"If you look hard enough at anything, you will find a 'yeah, but'. If you are consumed with failure, you will find a way to fail."

---

*D*o you know what a *"yabbit"* is?

[An abbreviation for a yellow rabbit?]

A *yabbit* is a person who uses the expression *"yeah, but"*, constantly, in every aspect of his or her life. These people are walking and talking excuse machines. They answer logic, truth and reality with "yeah but", followed by an excuse. If you look hard enough at anything, you will find a *"yeah, but"*. *If you are consumed with failure, you will find a way to fail.*

Golfers who make excuses for their poor play are yabbits. Perhaps the biggest yabbit is the golfer who instinctively knows which club to use on any given shot, but who says something like *"YEAH BUT the other guys are using 8-irons"*, or, *"YEAH BUT Tiger Woods wouldn't use a 5-wood here."* Yabbits look for reasons why they can't. *Yabbits are consumed with failure.*

This is what goes through the mind of a yabbit golfer as he or she goes around the golf course.

Yabbit Yabbit Yabbit Yabbit Yabbit Yabbit Yabbit Yabbit Yabbit
Yabbit Yabbit Yabbit Yabbit Yabbit Yabbit Yabbit Yabbit Yabbit
Yabbit Yabbit Yabbit Yabbit Yabbit Yabbit Yabbit Yabbit Yabbit
Yabbit Yabbit Yabbit Yabbit Yabbit Yabbit Yabbit Yabbit Yabbit
Yabbit Yabbit Yabbit Yabbit Yabbit Yabbit Yabbit Yabbit Yabbit
Yabbit Yabbit Yabbit Yabbit Yabbit Yabbit Yabbit Yabbit Yabbit
Yabbit Yabbit Yabbit Yabbit Yabbit Yabbit Yabbit Yabbit Yabbit
Yabbit Yabbit Yabbit Yabbit Yabbit Yabbit Yabbit Yabbit Yabbit
Yabbit Yabbit Yabbit Yabbit Yabbit Yabbit Yabbit Yabbit Yabbit
Yabbit Yabbit Yabbit Yabbit Yabbit Yabbit Yabbit
Yabbit Yabbit Yabbit Yabbit Yabbit Yabbit
Yabbit Yabbit Yabbit Yabbit Yabbit Yabbit
Yabbit Yabbit Yabbit Yabbit Yabbit
Yabbit Yabbit Yabbit Yabbit Yabbit
Yabbit Yabbit Yabbit Yabbit
Yabbit Yabbit Yabbit Yabbit
Yabbit Yabbit Yabbit
Yabbit Yabbit Yabbit
Yabbit Yabbit Yabbit
Yabbit Yabbit Yabbit
Yabbit Yabbit Yabbit
Yabbit Yabbit Yabbit Yabbit
Yabbit Yabbit Yabbit Yabbit
Yabbit Yabbit Yabbit Yabbit Yabbit
Yabbit Yabbit Yabbit Yabbit Yabbit Yabbit Yabbit

Are you a yabbit golfer?

Do you look for reasons
why you can't make a particular shot, or
why you can't improve?

Do you know the opposite of yeah but?

BUT YEAH

"People who say or think 'but yeah' are consumed with success and achievement"

---

he opposite of *yeah but* is *but yeah*.

[Clever!]

People who say or think "but yeah"

- look for reasons why they can

- are *consumed* with success and achievement

- are committed fully to the task at hand

- live full, rich, satisfying, successful lives

- have fun

- can't wait to get up in the morning

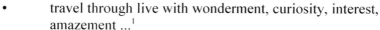

- travel through live with wonderment, curiosity, interest, amazement ...[1]

---

[1]   See page 124.

EXCEPTION OR RULE

"Undisciplined people ... pay attention to other people's opinions rather than living their own dreams."

---

eing a lawyer must be confusing because you are always looking for loop holes. You look for the exception to the rule.

In your life, do you live by the rule or do you look for the exception? The answer to this question is important in terms of the discipline required to maintain commitment in the face of the inevitable obstacles that you will face in life and golf. Undisciplined people, people who can't maintain a commitment, look for the exception. They make excuses. They make exceptions. They say "yeah but". They live "shoulda, coulda, woulda" lives. They pay attention to other people's opinions rather than living their own dreams.

Do you live by the exception or by the rule?

WHAT'S THE MATADOR GOT TO DO WITH GOLF?

"The matador has a plan and executes it.
Methodically and systematically, the matador
defeats the bull. Or he dies ... Defeat the bull or
die. And do it with excellence and integrity."

D *o you want to know what the matador's got to do*
with golf?

Close your eyes and picture that famous matador you
saw fight *el toro* in Madrid. See how he enters the bull ring.
Immaculately dressed. Proudly parading. Strutting. Totally in
control of his surroundings. The indisputable
champion of the bull-ring.

The matador has a plan and executes it.
Methodically and systematically, the
matador defeats the bull. Or he dies. The
matador cannot think about *how* to kill the
bull. He must do it. And do it with
honor. The matador cannot think about
technique. He must think only
about the target. Or he dies.
Like golf, bullfighting is a very
simple sport and the successful
matador understands his sport
perfectly:

Defeat the bull or die.
And do it with excellence and integrity.

The matador also knows that his actions and his thoughts are one. Each affect the other. And so, the matador is

purposefully
meticulous, disciplined, precise and confident.

Are you?

Think Good. Feel Good. Be Good.
Be Good. Feel Good. Think Good.

68

LOOK THE BULL IN THE EYES

"The matador welcomes his fear because fear is the fuel that energizes his efforts. Pressure is a tool."

---

 s the matador afraid? Of course he is afraid, *but he is not afraid of his fear.* The matador welcomes his fear because fear is the fuel that energizes his efforts. Pressure is a tool.

[Fear does cause the body to produce adrenalin. Hmmm.]

When the matador stands in the *plaza de toros* alone with the bull he has two choices: fight with courage, honor and pride or run in disgrace. You'll never see a matador run in disgrace. The matador knows that it is better to die in the fight rather than to retreat in fear.

The same with a golfer. When you stand up to the ball, look the bull in the eyes with *pundador*, which means strike the ball with courage and confidence. It won't always turn out the way you want, but you will feel better about yourself if you have hit it with courage and confidence because you will know in your heart that you did the best that you could possibly do.

When you hit the ball like a coward, with fear in your heart or in your mind, even if you hit a good shot, you lose your self-respect and your energy *recedes* so much that *The Needle* would not spin. If you are going to die, go out in style.[1]

The golf swing is meant to be executed by accelerating through the ball. When you are afraid, you tense up, try to steer the ball, hit tentatively, even decelerate through the ball. So stand tall, be proud, look the bull in the eyes and hit the ball like a matador.

Bull's-eye.

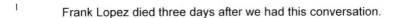

[1]   Frank Lopez died three days after we had this conversation.

DEFINING MOMENTS

"Usually, we don't recognize them as such until we look back at them."

---

*D*efining moments are those places in our lives when events turn sharply in a new direction. Usually, we don't recognize them as such until we look back at them.

One of the greatest feelings is being able to predict a defining moment in advance. Actually, one cannot do it with any real degree of accuracy, but "confidence" is *acting* like you can. Mohammed Ali's[1] pre-fight predictions are a classic example.

Let's say that you are in the finals of a match play tournament. Quietly predict that you are going to win and let your opponent and others know your prediction. If you don't win, they will forget about it, but if you do win, they will remember your prediction forever. Even better, so will you!

Look for the defining moments in your life.

---

[1] Actually, Cassius Clay's at the time.

WISH UPON A PAR

"If you've done IT once, you can do IT again."

You've been playing at your club for about 25 years. Have you parred every hole at least once?

[Yes.]

Do you believe that you could par any hole again?

[Yes.]

Of course. If you've done IT once, you can do IT again. But do you think that you can shoot par for an 18-hole round?

[No,]

You're right. If you think you can't, you won't.

[See, I told you.]

But if you think you can, you'd be right too. Do you get IT yet?

[You're really serious about actually consciously visualizing shooting 72.]

Si.

🎵 *When you wish upon a par ...* 🎵

BEEN THERE? DONE THAT? SO DO *IT* AGAIN!

"Burn IT into your mind."

---

ave you birdied every hole at your club at least once?

[Let me think. Yes, I believe I have.]

If you birdied every hole in the same round, what would your score be?

[54, but that's impossible.]

Impossible is a word that human beings use to explain what they don't, can't or don't want to understand. The point is that it doesn't matter whether it's possible or impossible. How many more times do I have to tell you this? *What matters is whether you believe IT could be possible.*

[Déjà vu.]

If you've birdied the hole once, then you can do IT again.

[Maybe if I get lucky.]

It's got nothing to do with getting lucky. You did IT once and therefore you can do IT again. And again. Of course if you

believe that you can't, then you won't. *Believe that you can do
IT again.* Consciously remember every good shot you've ever
had. Next time you make one of those shots, remember IT. *Burn
IT into your mind.* Every time you birdie a hole, file IT. If you
make a good decision, save IT.
Pretty soon you'll have your own
database of great shots, birdies, chip-ins,
crunched drives, drained putts, etc. In fact,
if you really think about it, your personal
database already exists.

Been There? Done That? Do IT Again!

[Been There? Done That? Do IT
Again is easy for you to say, but
it's not so easy to do.]

72

A PICTURE IS WORTH
1,000 WORDS,
MAYBE 1,000,000, OR MORE

*"The more images of YOU making great shots
that YOU can give YOUR brain to work with,
YOUR greater chance of success."*

Been There? Done That? Do IT Again *is easy to say,* but you
think that *it's not so easy to do.* You're right, but if you believe
that IT'S easy to do, then you would also be right.

[You keep saying that.]

Remember we talked about how the brain works? I don't know
whether it's more correct to say that mind and body are really
one, that the mind controls the body based upon the images that
are present in the mind, or simply that the mind processes
information and adjusts the body so quickly that
it just seems so. Whatever the answer, it
doesn't matter because picturing the
desired bodily result in your mind before
executing IT will give you the best
opportunity of actually doing IT.
There are no guarantees in life or in
golf. The best that you can do for
yourself is to give yourself the best
opportunity for success. Leave the
door open so if you happen to end up
in front of IT, you can walk through.

[How do I do that?]

Some people say you should do this before every shot, but I say do IT *throughout your round.*

[Do what?]

Search your personal database and recall every birdie that you have made on this hole, every time that you have struck a perfect shot like the next one you've got and every time that you've got an excellent result from a similar position. The more images of YOU making great shots that YOU can give YOUR brain to work with, YOUR greater chance of success.

At a subconscious level, your brain is constantly processing information, making thousands, maybe millions of minute adjustments to the various parts and systems of our bodies. As part of this process, every single bit of information that it receives (whether you are consciously aware of it or not) is compared instantly with every other bit of information it has ever received. Body language is an example of this process. Human beings subconsciously give clues about what they are thinking by their body position. Human beings also have the ability to receive this information, process it and act accordingly, all at a subconscious level. A momentary glance at a photograph of a man and woman enjoying a tropical vacation is a powerful stimulus that evokes all sorts of thoughts, memories and physical reactions.

[Especially in January in Toronto.]

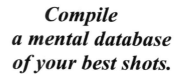

**Compile
a mental database
of your best shots.**

**Picture IT,
imagine what could be
and then let nature
take its course.**

COMPUTER GAMES

*"You have to make a conscious effort to tell
your computer what you want it to remember."*

I don't know too much about computers but I do know
that you have to make *a conscious effort* to tell your
computer what you want it to remember.

One good thing that you should program into your computer is
the feeling when you are standing behind your ball looking at a
straight-away, wide fairway, the type that extends perfectly
aligned like an extension of the tee-box. You have to admit that
it's pretty easy to get your alignment on this type of a shot.

Often, however, tee-boxes are angled and fairways bend and
curve. Sometimes it's difficult to feel comfortable with your
alignment. The trick is to call on your computer to remember
the thought of that straight-away, wide fairway, and then to find
the thought that sees this shot in the same way. The best way to
do this is to over-lay the computer-thought over the visual
thought and cause yourself to perceive the shot as a straight-
away shot. In other words, trick yourself into seeing, or thinking
you see a straight-away fairway. This technique works better if
you take a big, deep look at the fairway.

I MADE A MISTAKE. SO WHAT!

*"Golf is a game of mistakes. It's what you do
after the mistakes that shows in the score."*

Many years ago I saw you walking off the 18th green
after a match and I asked you, *"So how did you
play?"*

You said, *"I won, but I made four mistakes."*

Four mistakes, Juan, only four mistakes in 18 holes, I'd say
that's pretty good. Golf is a game of
mistakes. *It's what you do after the
mistakes that shows in the score.* A
golf match takes four to five hours to
play, often coming down to the last few
holes. That's a lot of time to learn from
your mistakes and correct them.

Golf gives you many chances to redeem
yourself. If you are aware of your mistakes
and learn from them, you can *use* them to
keep *your focus* throughout the match. For
example, if you missed a short putt because
you didn't hit it firmly enough, remember
what you want to do on the next short
putt. *Burn IT* into your mind and then
get on with your next shot.

You'll get your chances, don't worry.

PICKING UP VS. GIVING UP

"Your friends were confusing having a good time on a golf course with having a good time playing golf."

I remember you telling me about your game with two friends who simply gave up after they had a few bad holes and started acting really silly, calling themselves Hans and Franz. The excuses that they gave you were funny. *"We didn't give up. We changed our priorities mid-round. We lost our zeal for shooting a good score. We just wanted to have fun. It just sort of got to a point where we were tired."*

They gave up and couldn't or wouldn't admit it. Your friends were confusing *having a good time on a golf course* with *having a good time playing golf.* They gave up having a good time playing golf for simply having a good time on the golf course.

'TIL DEATH DO YOU PART

"Be fearlessly and fully committed to every shot."

B *e committed* to every shot. *Be fully committed* to every shot. *Be fearlessly and fully committed* to every shot. Once the matador decides on the pass he will make, he is committed. Once you make up your mind about the shot that you want to make, make that shot.

If you decide that you are going to play a lob wedge over the bunker to land softly on the narrow green, *be committed* to that shot. You've made it before and you can and will make it again if you are committed to making it. If you have the slightest doubt about the shot, don't make it. Doubt means that you are not committed. Being committed means that you have no doubts.

Be committed to every shot as if you were married to IT.

Be committed to every shot as if IT was the last shot that you will ever take.

Be committed to every shot as if your life depended on IT.

Be committed to every shot as if the whole universe consisted of YOU and IT.

Be committed to every shot 'til death do you part.

THE GREEN IS WAITING FOR YOU

"Shyly seductive, it shows off the softness of its slopes, contours and textures. Secretly hot-tempered and demanding, it taunts you, just by being there. Waiting. For you."

T he Green is waiting for you. Faithful. Dependable. Lonely. The Green is waiting for you.

Today, as the shadows of dusk are long, go to The Green slowly and watch it waiting. For you. Shyly seductive, it shows off the softness of its slopes, contours and textures. Secretly hot-tempered and demanding, it taunts you, just by being there. Waiting. For you.

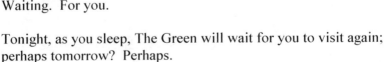

Now touch it. Sense its life. Full of life, but tired-life, spent, having done its job today. Being The Green. For You. Just for you. Calm. Content. Tired. Alive. Waiting. For you.

Tonight, as you sleep, The Green will wait for you to visit again; perhaps tomorrow? Perhaps.

Alone, The Green waits for you. Feel its loneliness.

78

THE TIME ZONES
OF YOUR LIFE

"What time it is for you depends on where you live."

If three golfers were teeing off simultaneously in Toronto, Calgary and Vancouver, what would their tee-off times be?

[3:27 p.m. in Toronto, 1:27 p.m. in Calgary and
12:27 p.m. in Vancouver.]

Did you know that China spans five continental time zones, but within China, there is only one time zone?

[What's *that* got to do with
golf?]

What time it is for you depends on where you live. Just like there are different time zones all over the world, *there are different time zones in your life.*

For example, people who live in the present, live in the "what is" time zone. People who live in the past, live in the "what was" time zone, etc.

Where do you live?

157

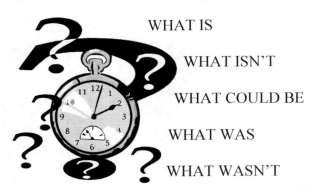

WHAT IS

WHAT ISN'T

WHAT COULD BE

WHAT WAS

WHAT WASN'T

WHAT SHOULD BE

WHAT SHOULDN'T BE

WHAT COULD HAVE BEEN

WHAT WOULD HAVE BEEN

WHAT SHOULDN'T HAVE BEEN

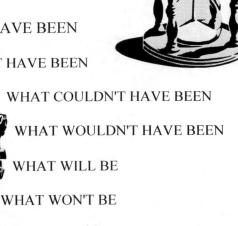

WHAT COULDN'T HAVE BEEN

WHAT WOULDN'T HAVE BEEN

WHAT WILL BE

WHAT WON'T BE

WHAT SHOULDN'T BE

WHAT COULDN'T BE

WHERE DO YOU LIVE?

79

BULL SHOULD

"In life and in golf, your success will be determined by how well you recognize what is and what isn't, and imagine what could be."

O nly three of the time zones of your life have any value, what are they?

[Tell me.]

What is, what isn't and what could be. *What is* and *what isn't* are reality. *What could* be are your dreams. In life and in golf, your success will be determined by how well you *recognize* what is and what isn't, and *imagine* what could be. Forget about the other time zones. It's the stuff people think about who haven't figured out that you can't predict the future or change the past.

Let me say it another way. If you are present in Toronto, but living on Mountain Standard Time, you are going to miss a good part of the day. *You are out of sync with your surroundings.* If you live a *shoulda, coulda, woulda* life, you are going to miss a good part of your life!

[What's *this* got to do with *golf*?]

How many times, for example, have you heard a golfer complain about tee-boxes or tee-markers that are misaligned to the fairway? This golfer is thinking about *what should be* and ignoring *what is.*

The successful golfer accepts what is,
thinks about what could be
and then lets IT happen.

Focus on what could be.

Golf is a game of is and am,
not a game of shoulda, coulda, woulda.

Where is the ball going to go?

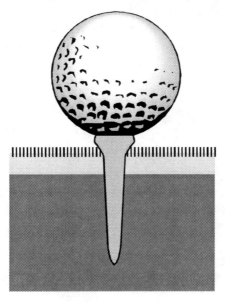

What club am I going to use?

80

TUNE YOUR SPIRIT

"Spiritual dissonance is what happens when we have an internal conflict, or when we live in contradiction or dissonance with reality ... and your health, your well being, your peace of mind and most of all, your performance will be affected."

I t has always amazed me how a piano tuner tunes a piano, by ear, listening for the *dissonant vibration* of out-of-tune piano strings.

Spiritual dissonance is what happens when we have an internal conflict, or when we live in contradiction or dissonance with reality. *Out of sync.* Your subconscious will recognize this dissonant vibration, and your health, your well being, your peace of mind and, most of all, your performance will be affected.

There's a lot of wisdom in the ancient philosophies that talk about balance and balancing the forces and energies of the body and the universe. If you act differently than you feel, if you speak differently than you think, if you live differently than you are, you live a life of contradiction; you live in a state of disharmony.

[What's *that* got to do with *golf*?]

Remember how I told you how simply by thinking a thought, your body automatically adjusts. If you want to hit the ball in the middle of the fairway but you are thinking about out of bounds, your mind and body get out of sync, and you know the result. It's like a shadow of yourself separates and aims out of bounds. You are not whole. There is a contradiction. Your *energy* is divided. You become weak and ineffective because you are giving your control centre conflicting messages.

ARE YOU IN TUNE WITH REALITY?

ARE *YOU* YOUR HANDICAP?

"Some golfers sabotage their own game so well, they should be arrested and charged with treason."

---

re *you* your handicap?

[What's the difference between an orange?]

An orange and what?

[Never mind, it's got nothing to do with golf. What do you mean, am I my handicap?]

You've heard people talk about course management as a technique for lowering your scores. I say the key is *self-management*. Many golfers are their own biggest handicap. Some golfers sabotage their own game so well, they should be arrested and charged with treason.

Are YOU your handicap?

163

THE HAWK AND THE SHARK

"I'm doing this because I can. I am The Hawk."

o you want to know how to get into The Zone?

[Yes.]

Think about The Hawk and The Shark.

[No, the golfing Zone, you know that *place of intense and concentrated focus where the energy of passion, fear and enthusiasm is transformed into strength and singularity of purpose.*][1]

I know what you mean and I still say think about The Hawk and The Shark.

The Hawk is a majestic bird. Proudly and patiently, it sits waiting to pounce on its prey. Gracefully and effortlessly it glides into the wind as if to say:

"I'm doing this because I can. I am The Hawk."

---

[1]   See Chapter 65 of *Golf Is a Very Simple Game*.

The Shark is a predator. Its purpose is to eat so it can live to eat. Black, cold, icy eyes reveal no conscience, no opinion, no judgments, no demons. Sudden, vicious, definite and deadly are words that describe how The Shark hunts.

The Shark and The Hawk live in The Zone.

83

MORE ZONE

*"In The Zone, you are connected to the wisdom
and the performance of all of the greatest
human achievements. In The Zone, you are
connected with 'truth'."*

---

e think our bodies are sharply defined by the outer
layer of our skin, but that's *just the part that we
can see.*

[Frank, you're getting weird again.]

Our bodies are vibrating energy, just like everything in the
universe is vibrating energy. Only
part of this energy is visible to
humans. Radio waves, ultra
violet waves from the sun and
body heat are examples of
invisible energy. Your skin is
just the end of the *visible* part
of YOUR vibrating energy, but
YOU extend past your skin.

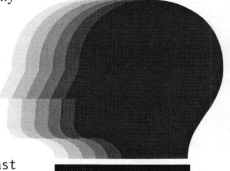

[Then, everyone extends past
their skins too.]

Exactly, but not just every*one*, every*thing's* vibrations extend
similarly. The Zone is where these vibrations hang out, so to
speak. YOUR consciousness is part of the vibrating energy
associated with your "body". *The Zone is the collective
consciousness of the energy of the universe.*

We are connected to and with every other thing that has ever lived, is living and that will ever live. We are part of something much bigger. On a molecular level, we breathe air molecules that used to be in someone else. Everything we eat used to be part of something else, etc. In fact, many of our thoughts are thoughts that were once thoughts of others. At a conscious level, we are only aware of the vibrations of our individual human experience, but quietly, automatically and naturally, *we are "tuned into" the vibrating energy of the universe.*

Being in The Zone is fine tuning your consciousness beyond

your ordinary human consciousness. It's like tuning into a secret radio hidden within your radio. In The Zone, you have no past, no memories, no language. There just IS. Energy exists and vibrates. Absolutely no interference. None of the ordinary distractions of the normal human consciousness. *In The Zone, you are connected to the wisdom and the performance of all of the greatest human achievements.* In The Zone, you are connected with "truth". In The Zone, you are both deeply aware of, and detached from the moment. In The Zone, you are what could be.

[How do I get there?]

By believing that The Zone exists and deciding to go there.

[That's it?]

84

MORE ABOUT AUTOMATIC GOLFER

"You don't 'get to' automatic golfer. Automatic golfer happens because IT is you. "

I told you about automatic golfer,[1] which is a place where you let the shot happen. Automatic golfer is trusting your internal computer to repeat earlier successes automatically. You know and you do. I know you are thinking *"How can I get to this place called automatic golfer?"*

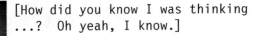

[How did you know I was thinking ...? Oh yeah, I know.]

Juan, turn off the tape machine for a minute and then turn it back on in 10 seconds.

[Okay.]

When you did that, I am sure that you didn't have to think about every single movement that you made. You just thought *"turn off the tape machine"* and you did it automatically. If you had to consciously decide to do everything that was required for you to turn off the tape machine, you'd never be able to do it. The same thing with a golf shot. You want to imagine the shot, and then you want to proceed to do IT with no further thought, internal discussion or effort. You want to say to yourself *"hit this shot"* and then do IT.

---

[1]   See chapter 35 of *Golf Is a Very Simple Game*

[Golf really is a very simple game! Right.]

The link that connects your body and your mind is your nervous system. An incredibly complex "tree" of nerves. Every time you do or think anything new, your internal computer system creates a program that it can run for future use. For example, fear is a learned response. You can be afraid even if there is no actual danger, just by believing that danger is present. Just by thinking about a dangerous situation, the "fear program" in your mind runs and you feel afraid. All of this happens automatically, instinctively and involuntarily.

You don't "get to" automatic golfer. Automatic golfer *happens* because *IT is you*. Just like breathing, eating, walking and sleeping "happen" to you as a human being, automatic golfer is part of your experience as a human golfer. IT is what YOU are NOW. IT happens and IT will happen. Automatically. There is no *effort*, no *trying* to experience automatic golfer. IT happens. IT is.

On the other hand, automatic golfer is not, *not-trying*, because the act of *not-trying* is a conscious effort. *Automatic golfer is being.*

In automatic golfer, even a distant fleeting awareness of your objective is enough to achieve results. In fact, being too aware of your objective is no good. For example, let's say you are hungry and you see food. You simply eat it. There is no great effort to do so. No great plan. No effort. No trying. You are aware of hunger and you eat. As you tee-up your ball, you simply do IT.

You choose the appropriate spot and tee it up. No great plan. No effort.
No trying. Simply execution. You are aware that your objectives are to get the ball into the hole in the fewest number of strokes and to enjoy the game that you are playing.

The shot is simply part of this process.

Part of YOU.

Part of IT.

85

WHAT
WERE YOU THINKING ABOUT?

*"You don't have to think HOW TO DO golf
...You CAN just DO golf."*

 remember you tol' me about a match that you played and how the difference came down to three fairly easy shots that you didn't make. *What were you thinking about?*

[The shot.]

Think hard.

[Well, the first shot was a sidehill-uphill shot, so I was thinking that the ball would tend to hook so I should compensate ...]

Mechanics, Juan, mechanics. You were thinking *how* instead of *where*. You knew how to make those shots. You've *learned* them, *practiced* them and *made* them hundreds of times.

You don't have to think HOW TO DO golf. Do you have to think how to walk, how to throw a ball or how to ride a bike? NO! You learned how to do it and you just DO it. Can you imagine if the average person thought about walking, the way that the average golfer thinks about making a golf shot? *"OK now, slowly shift your weight onto the left leg until it's about 75*

percent over your left foot, then as you move forward and your
left thigh tenses, bend your right foot at the joints of the toes ..."
No, you don't think this when you are walking because you
know how to walk. You learned how to do it and you just DO it.
You just walk.

Automatically. Instinctively. Involuntarily.

You CAN just DO golf.
Believe IT.

Thinking HOW, won't do IT.
Think WHERE, and DO IT.

FEEL THE RIGHT CLUB

"Let yourself choose the right club."

---

*Y*ou know how sometimes you are thinking about what club to use and it just feels like a certain club, but a voice in your head tells you it can't be that club because, for example, last time you played the hole, you used a different club?

The *feeling* you had is the signal from your computer, *announcing* the correct club, having instantly taken into consideration all of the relevant factors including every shot that you have ever taken. The *voice* is a demon that lives in all of us. Be aware of those feelings. They are your friends. Learn to recognize them and succeed. Listen to the demon and fail.

Here's a good way to let yourself choose the right club. First, narrow the choices down to two clubs. Then, take the two clubs, one in each hand and wait until you get the signal. If you ask your subconscious to give you the right answer, IT will tell you. You know what club is the right club to hit. Don't interfere with your own automatic processes. *Let yourself* choose the right club.

Pick the club that feels right.
Trust IT.

WINNING

"Winning begins with your physical and mental preparation, long before you tee-off on the first hole."

---

n any competition, there can only be one winner, but there doesn't have to be a loser.

[You're talking in circles again.]

There's a difference between not winning, and losing. There's no shame in not winning. If it's someone else's day, you can't prevent not winning, but you can do something about losing.

Winning a golf match or tournament is a process. It is not simply sinking your last putt on the 18th hole. Winning begins with your physical and mental preparation, long before you tee-off on the first hole. In fact, the physical part of your preparation should be overshadowed by the mental preparation.

Mental preparation includes having a plan both of your overall style of play, and the way that you are going to play each hole. Is it medal or match play? Are you going to play aggressively, or conservatively, waiting for your opponent to make a mistake? Mental preparation includes actually sitting down with a pen and a paper and planning each hole. Mental preparation for winning includes preparing yourself for the inevitable ups and downs of a round of golf. You will remind yourself to expect some shots that don't meet your expectations and that these shots, like all shots, are opportunities for greatness.

Just like a pilot has a checklist that he or she goes over before the flight, you can do the same thing before you go into automatic golfer mode. You will arrive at the course with plenty of time to do your pre-round preparation including descending into The Zone about 30 to 45 minutes before your tee-off time. During the warm-up, you will practice the scoring shots that will be most important for you that day: putting, chipping, lob wedge, pitching wedge and then a few drivers and iron shots. All the while, you are running over your checklist of mechanical matters so that you don't have to think about them again.

TIPTOE ON A RAZOR BLADE

"Being mentally ready for peak performance is a razor-thin state of mind bordered by fear and confidence."

Being mentally ready for peak performance is a razor-thin state of mind bordered by fear and confidence. In fact, the blade of the razor is not where the two states of mind *meet*, but where they *overlap and mix*.

Step to the right, and fear creates tension and apprehension. Step to the left and overconfidence causes you to assume that you will make your shots.

Tiptoeing on the razor blade gives you just the right mixture of fear and confidence so that you can *let* yourself make the shot.

SENSE THE BIG PICTURE

*"Precision and accuracy require minute
adjustments in the midst of performance that are
impossible if you are tense."*

I
've told you many times that golf is a game of precision
and accuracy, not strength. Precision and accuracy
require minute adjustments in the midst of performance
that are impossible if you are
tense.

*Relax. Let IT
happen. You know*
how to do IT.
Engage automatic
golfer. *Believe* that
you are in automatic
golfer mode. *Sense* the
big picture. If you get too
specific, you tense up. If you
are chipping, *make sure* you get it
on the green, focus on the big picture.

Trust that you will get it close.
You will!

GET OUT OF YOUR OWN WAY: GET YOURSELF TOGETHER

"Stand tall, be proud like a matador and hit it."

Pay attention to all of the things that you are thinking about throughout a round of golf. Seriously, make a list and review it at the end of the round.

[I bet I'll be surprised.]

You'll be shocked. Sometimes, when you stand over the ball, it's as if part of you jumps out of your body, stands in front of you on the tee and starts a conversation about all of the bad things that *could* happen; the mechanics of your swing, your office, your car, your family; anything and everything *other than* getting the ball into the hole in the fewest number of strokes.

Get out of your own way.

Get yourself together.

Stand tall, be proud like a matador and hit it.

YOU CAN'T ARGUE
WITH THE DEMONS

*"Their whole purpose is to get you into a
discussion, perhaps even an argument with
yourself."*

---

o you know why you can't argue with the demons?

Because their whole purpose is to get you into a
discussion, perhaps even an argument with yourself.

For example, let's say that you are
really tired, thirsty and feeling
weak, the demons will try to get
you into a discussion with
yourself about how tired, thirsty
and weak you are. Once you get
into that discussion, they exit, mission
accomplished. Before you know
it, you have left your first putt
on the 2nd sudden-victory hole
12 feet short, giving yourself an

"opportunity for
greatness" that you would
have been much better off
avoiding.

Some of the demons are
indecision, hesitation, self-
doubt, uncertainty,
distrust, apprehension,

disbelief, cynicism, pessimism, unhappiness, misery, gloom, dejection, disappointment, shame, discouragement, depression, insecurity, tension, anxiety, confusion, despair, fear, worry, panic, defeat, deflation, letdown, failure, frustration, futility, hopelessness, pressure, stress, nervousness, impatience, jitters, embarrassment, giving in, losing hope, quitting, faze, torment, devastation, desperation, gloom, fluster, exasperation.

Your friends are confidence, faith, patience, poise, purpose, belief, cheerfulness, composure, determination, enthusiasm, intensity, conviction, passion, desire, energy, concentration, attention, care, love, spirit, thrill, vigor, eagerness, anticipation, excitement, hope, motivation, resolve, self-assurance, tenacity, diligence, perseverance, grace, presence, posture, attitude, composure, coolness, dignity, elegance, finesse, grace, serenity, ambition, courage, boldness, respect, delight, courtesy,

The phrases *what if, yeah but* and *if I could only,* are demon speak

ALWAYS FINISH
WITH THREE *GREAT* SHOTS

"It's important to punctuate the end of a round with success."

---

fter each round, make a point of carrying out some sort of ritual that involves making three *great* shots even if the three shots are short putts dead into the hole.

[That sounds pretty dumb.]

I know you think this is a dumb idea, but it's not. It's important to punctuate the end of a round with success. This helps you maintain your confidence. Athletic rituals are important because they give you permission to play the game. For example, you told me that in hockey, you always put on your right skate first. Why?

[I'll break my leg if I don't.]

Exactly. Do you see my point?

[Not really.]

Athletic rituals help organize the butterflies that precede competition, and maintain confidence and enthusiasm between competitions.

WHY DO I FALL APART
ON THE BACK NINE?

*"Because you think there is such a thing as the
back nine."*

I heard that your friends at the club call you "Mr. Front
Nine".

[Yeah, I usually fall apart on
the back nine. Why do I do that?]

Because you think there is such a thing as
the back nine.

[Huh?]

What do you think about after you've
finished nine holes?

[Well, I look at the score and see how
I did. If I shot a good score, I
hope that I can keep it together. If
I shot a bad score, then I try to
gather my composure so I can shoot
a good score for the back nine to
salvage a respectable score for
the 18.]

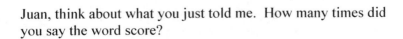

Juan, think about what you just told me. How many times did
you say the word score?

[Two or three.]

Five times, I counted. I ask you one simple question, and you say the word score five times. Do you see what you are thinking about after nine holes? Why don't you let someone else keep score and tell them you don't want to know your score until you have finished your round?

[Then I wouldn't know how I was playing.]

No. You mean, you wouldn't know how you scored for the first nine holes. You're stuck on this front nine, back nine thing. If you were thinking about one shot at a time, you'd know exactly how you were playing and the score wouldn't matter!

If you only had time to play three holes and you scored three birdies, what would you think?

[I'd want to play the other 15 holes.]

Exactly. You couldn't accept that playing three holes in three-under par was an excellent result. You focus on your scores for nine or 18 holes as a measurement of how you are playing and have no frame of reference smaller than nine holes. No wonder you fall apart on the back nine.

Golf is a game that is played one shot at a time, but most golfers *perceive and believe* that golf is an 18-hole game divided into two nine-hole segments. The problem is that dividing the round into two nine-hole segments gives the demons anxiety, fear and hopelessness, an opportunity to go to work.

As you are playing the game, you can think about the shot, or you can think about the score. Thinking about the shot gives you the best opportunity to achieve a good score. Thinking about the score takes your mind off the shot, creates a continuous level of anxiety and is more likely to result in a psychological let down if you have a bad hole.

Thinking about the shot keeps you in the game, throughout the game, however long it happens to be that day.

94

PLAY THREE HOLE ROUNDS

"It's like a company issuing quarterly financial statements."

---

*R*emember when you learned Transcendental Meditation? You wouldn't tell me your mantra.

`[Sorry, but they told me I couldn't tell anyone.  Anyway, I paid $400 for it.]`

I think you overpaid because repetition of any sound or thought will produce the same effect. Relaxation and concentration. Transcending consciousness into a deeper state of being.

Meditators use a *mantra* to transcend the conscious state and get into a zone. Repetition of the *mantra* diverts the mind from the conscious state of making things happen, to the transcendental state of being. Meditators will tell you that one of the benefits of meditation is increased ability to focus. Meditators usually meditate for let's say 20 to 30 minutes at a time, whereas golfers are expected to focus for four to five hours at a time. Most golfers need more than a *mantra* to help keep them focused and in The Zone.

One thing that you can do to help maintain your focus is to break down your 18-hole round into

six three-hole rounds. It's like a company issuing quarterly financial statements. Set a goal as to the number under or over par that you want to be in each three hole round and then see what happens. This works for many reasons.

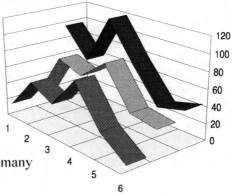

- It gives you a goal that more often than not you can achieve, therefore enjoying success throughout your round.

- It dampens the effect of a bad hole. For example, let's say that you are a bogey golfer and you set your three-hole total of three over par. Even if you were to get a double bogey on the first hole, you can still reach your goal with par and bogey on the next two holes. Even if you don't reach your goal and you have three double bogeys, you get the opportunity to start all over again on the next three holes, there putting the last three holes out of your mind.

- You get much quicker and more constant feedback about your overall performance.

- You give yourself permission to put a bad shot or a bad hole behind you.

95

A FISTFUL OF JELL-O:
WHEN THE WHEELS FALL OFF

"Just as in life, your golf will eventually get better."

---

hat can you do when the wheels fall off?

[Some days my golf is so bad, I wonder if I will ever hit a decent shot again!]

Golf mirrors life and just as you have ups and downs in your life, good days and bad days, it's the same with golf. Just as in life, your golf will eventually get better. When the wheels fall off, it's time to go back to the basics. Here's five things that you can think about:

- Keep the ball in play and play safe.

- Be patient and enjoy other things.

- Put the bad club away completely for a while and play with the club in which you have the most confidence.

- Play a completely different game[1].

- Accept that "Salvage Operations" are in progress.

---

[1]   See chapter 37.

CAREER ROUND 18ᵀᴴ HOLE

*"Every shot is a unique event and deserves the
same thought, consideration, deliberation and
execution as every other shot that you take."*

The career round 18th hole is a mysterious and two-
faced temptress. She usually looks so friendly,
especially when you've conquered most, if not all of
her brothers and sisters. However, often, it's like
there's an invisible elastic membrane that covers this 18th hole,
keeping you from breaking through to the next ability plateau.
Any golfer that's taken a double or triple bogey (or even worse
like you did) on a
career round
18th hole
knows what
I'm
talking
about.

*So Juan,
what can you do so that
next time you are four over after 17, you don't take a quadruple
bogey nine on such an easy par five?* Worse, yet Juan, you took
seven strokes to get down from 160 yds. I guess, a chip out, a
lost ball in the hazard, another hazard shot and then a bunker
shot can do that.

**There's a difference between being aware of the score
and being obsessed with the score.**

Think back Juan, you were always aware of the score, but once you got the two birdies on 15 and 17 you were thinking only about the score. In fact, on the 18th tee, you were not only celebrating your birdie on the 17, you were celebrating what you thought would be a certain career round. Four over par after 17 and you could bogey 18 with your eyes closed; double-bogey it playing upside-down. But, instead of thinking about your next shot, you were thinking about who you were going to tell about your great score and looking around for me to see where I was.

The 18th hole on a career round is where you must focus on each shot and only the shot at hand. Once you start making *assumptions* that you will make any shot you take, regardless of the difficulty of the shot, you are in trouble. You tol' me that in law, you never assume anything because when you do that, you make an *ass* out of *u* and *me*. Every shot is a unique event and deserves the same thought, consideration, deliberation and execution as every other shot that you take. What you did was get wrapped up in the score and in your performance the last 17 holes, and then *assumed* that that would be enough to get you in with par, or at worst, a bogey on the 18th.

Guess what Juan? You didn't make an ass out of *me* by taking a quadruple bogey on the 18th!

MAKE YOUR LAST THOUGHT
A SMILE

*"You will hit the ball with more confidence and
your swing will be strong and fluid."*

Sometimes I see you go through your pre-shot routine
with confidence and discipline, but lose that confident
spirit just after you take your stance. I can see it in
your face because you get this very serious look,
almost a tense frown. When this happens, I can almost predict
that your swing will be stiff and quick.

I don't know why, but I do know that smiling does something,
not just to your face, but to your body and to your spirit. Make
your last thought a smile and see what happens. You won't hit a
perfect shot every time, no one can do this, but you will hit the
ball with more confidence and your swing will be strong and
fluid.

Go the whole round with a smile on your face and see what
happens.

98

PRECISION + DISCIPLINE
= EXCELLENCE + SUCCESS

"Golf is a game of precision and discipline."

O ne thing that we often seem to forget is that missing a short putt, carelessly taken, is as much as a "penalty" as pulling your ball out of a hazard. Golf is a game of precision and discipline. In fact, you can't possibly be precise, if you are not disciplined. Precision and discipline go together - a formula:

discipline + precision =
excellence + success

One place where discipline and precision are required is on your short putts. A short putt is always either the result of missing the previous putt or making a good shot from off the green. Either way, your don't want to get caught up in your disappointment of missing the putt, or drunk with the success of your good approach or chip shot. You need the discipline to take your time and perform your pre-putt routine, and of course, the precision to putt the ball into the hole. If you care about your score, leave the one-handed, back-hand walking and the straddle-stance putts at home! Stand tall, be proud, and confidently stroke the ball into the hole. Tell yourself that you are the best putter in the world. Aim for the bottom of the hole.

Watch it go in.

99

CLEAN YOUR CLUBS
AND SHINE YOUR PUTTER

"Looking good makes you feel good."

I f Think Good, Feel Good, Be Good is an equation, Look Good fits in there too. Looking good makes you feel good. I don't care who you are. Looking good says *"I care. I'm meticulous. I'm proud. I'll take the time I need to do what I have to do."*

To whom is "looking good" speaking?

`[If you call me grasshopper ...]`

"Looking Good" is speaking first to yourself, and then to your opponent. Make sure that you dress and carry yourself so *YOU think* that you look good. Other peoples' tastes vary, so please yourself. Once you start thinking, "I care" then you are on your way.

One more thing. Clean your clubs and shine your putter. Now you are talking to your opponent and the golf course and telling both of them that you are in charge, that you have all of the details under control and that you are ready to take care of business.

HAVE FUN

100

AM I GOING TO HAVE FUN REGARDLESS OF WHATEVER HAPPENS ON THE GOLF COURSE?

"Do you always think about playing 36?"

---

o you love playing golf?

Do you look forward to waking up in the morning so that you can play?

Do you arrange your personal and business affairs around your golf game?

Do you love the smell of freshly mown grass?

Do you say "hi" to the back shop guys?

Do you love to play golf because it is a game?

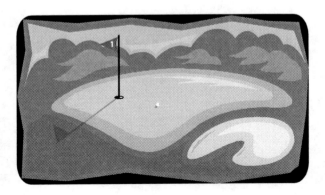

194

Do you try to be the first golfer to arrive at the course?

Do you like your golf ball or hate it?

After a bad shot, can you say to yourself "that's interesting"?

Is there any greater sight than to see
your ball sitting up on a juicy fairway?

As you shake hands with your playing partners as you walk off
the 18th green, are you disappointed that the round is over?

Do you always think about playing 36?

Do you yell "Oh Baby!" after your opponent
drains a 25-footer to save par and tie the hole?

Do you putt-out a conceded putt just because you love hearing the sound of your ball dropping into the cup?

101

HOW ARE YOU
GOING TO LIVE YOUR LIFE
WHILE YOU ARE WAITING
TO DIE?

"I know how I am going to live my life while I'm waiting to die, how are you going to live yours?"

H ow are YOU going to live YOUR life while YOU are waiting to die?

[What kind of a question is that?]

It's a good question, something you should think about now.

[I've learned a lot from the way that you have lived your life, but even more importantly, about how you are living your life while you are waiting to die.]

We are all waiting to die, Juan. Life is waiting to die. The only difference in my case now is that I have a pretty good idea when it is going to happen. In terms of the universe and the history of everything, the difference that I have remaining in my life and the difference that you have remaining in yours, is barely distinguishable. I know how I am going to live my life while I'm waiting to die, how are you going to live yours?

LIVE EXCELLENCE
AND HAVE FUN

EPILOGUE

102

THE LAST CONVERSATION

"You do your part and I'll do mine?"

I'll never forget my last conversation with my friend Frank Lopez:

Juan, I am going to die soon. I need you to make me two promises.

[What are they?]

You always said that I was the only person that could teach you, but there is another teacher. Just tell yourself that you are ready to meet him and he'll appear. Allow him to be your teacher. He is wise and educated. You are not being disloyal.

[I guess I could do that. What else?]

You might think I'm crazy, but I need you to buy something called an Aurameter.

[An Aurameter? What's an Aurameter?]

An Aurameter is a dowsing device which is used to detect various forms of energy. I know it's difficult for you to accept right now, but if you'll get the Aurameter, you'll understand what I'm talking about.

[Where do I get one?]

200

You'll find it, and when you do, learn how to use it. Then, I want you to test my personal belongings that I leave my family.

[Test your personal belonging?   For what?]

For my energy.

[Frank, what ...?]

Juan, you ask too many questions.

You do your part and I'll do mine.

103

EPILOGUE

*"Did this force have anything to do with
my dead friend's energy?"*

I n the summer of 1996, as I was writing *Golf Is a Very Simple Game: The Golf Teachings of the Late Señor Francisco Lopez,* I visited Frank's brother Emilio and his wife Laura. As a tribute to Frank, they have Frank's furniture set up in their basement as almost a virtual replica of various rooms in Frank's house.

Walking down the basement stairs for the first time, once again I felt a definite presence, a force, if you will, tangible and real, like what happens when you push two similarly-poled magnets together. The closer I got to Frank's possessions, especially his golf clubs, the feeling intensified.

Thinking that perhaps I had imagined this experience, or made the feelings happen, I made a mental note to return with my wife after the summer vacation.

Two weeks later, while looking for a lunch stop, we found ourselves parked in front of the American Dowsing Society's book store in St. Johnsbury, Vermont. The truth is that I didn't remember Frank's last words to me as I entered the store, but they thundered in my head as soon as I saw it:

An Aurameter.

Upon our return home, I visited Laura and Emilio again, this time with my wife, Shelley. She too felt the energy. Strong, distinct and very real. We noticed that it seemed to travel around the room. First intense, then diminishing until we moved to a different area. In a way, it was eerie. In a way, uplifting.

Standing in front of Frank's picture of a matador, the Aurameter bent toward it with a significant and noticeable pull, as if to say *"Good idea about the matador, huh?"* The same thing happened near Frank's golf clubs, near his chess set and near a photograph of a close and beloved relative.

Did this force have anything to do with my dead friend's energy?

I believe it did. *Do you?*

I hope you enjoyed this book.

Jonathan Fine

FRANCISCO (FRANK) LOPEZ

Frank Lopez was a great golf teacher.

Born in Spain in 1945, young Frank learned to play golf as a caddy at the Real Club de Golf in Prat de Llobragat, a suburb of Barcelona.

As a caddie for Canadian touring professional Stan Leonard in the Canada [now World Cup] Cup matches in Barcelona, 13-year old Frank told Leonard *"some day, I will come to America to play."*

True to his word, traveling to North America as a teenager in search of golfing opportunities, Frank worked first in Glen Ridge Country Club in New Jersey, and then settled in Toronto in 1969, working at Rosedale Golf Club, Oakdale Golf and Country Club and Streetsville Glen Golf Club.

Frank Lopez was a great golf teacher. So much so that members of golf clubs where Frank had taught would insist that Frank continue to teach them, even making private appointments at local driving ranges on his day off.

Educated in life, Frank had a deep insight into the psychology of the human mind. Frank understood instinctively that an image was worth a 1000 words of instruction and therefore would tell students to "stand tall, be proud like a matador and hit it", rather than getting into the intricate and confusing details of the sequential bending, twisting and straightening various body parts.

Frank Lopez died April 9, 1992 at the age of 47.

JONATHAN FINE

J onathan Fine is the senior partner of the Toronto law firm Fine & Deo and is recognized nationally as a leading litigator in the field of Condominium Law. In addition to practicing and teaching law for over 20 years, Mr. Fine has contributed articles to various publications and hosted live television talk-shows originating out of Toronto.

Mr. Fine has also been a student of motivation and success and created the personal development seminar *Stand Tall, Be Proud and Hit It*. He lives in Toronto with his wife Shelley and four children.

What's This Got To Do With Golf? is the second in a series of books sub-titled *The Golf Teachings Of The Late Señor Francisco Lopez.*

**GOLF
IS A
VERY
SIMPLE
GAME**

*The Golf Teachings
of the
Late Señor Francisco Lopez
Vol. I*

ABOUT *Golf Is A Very Simple Game:*
The Golf Teachings of the Late Señor Francisco Lopez
Vol I.

Acclaimed internationally as a masterpiece and compared to all of the golf classics, *Golf Is A Very Simple Game: The Golf Teachings of the Late Señor Francisco Lopez,* is based upon proven psychological principles of success and motivation.

"- one of the most talked about books ... of the 1990's"
- The Financial Post

This is not just another "how to" golf instruction book, but rather an inspirational story, indeed a life-philosophy. You could almost sub-title the book: *How to Succeed in Anything.*

"*Golf Is A Very Simple Game: The Golf Teachings of the Late Señor Francisco Lopez*, is the masterpiece. It is rivaled only by Harvey Penick's *Little Red Book*, which until I read yours, was my classic."
-Ben Jackson, Golf Professional,
Stonington C.C.,
Stonington Connecticut

After reading this book, a golfer can't help but be inspired because it gives the reader permission to be humanly imperfect and excel. In short, live your life and play your golf with excellence.

"An essential read in order to get to the winner's circle!"

-Pauline Kelly,
Motivational Coach and
Former All-American Golf Team Member

Many golfers might challenge the message of the provocative title of this book, but through his student and friend Jonathan Fine, the late golf professional Frank Lopez reminds us that golf is both simple, and a game: *get the ball into the hole in the fewest number of strokes and have fun doing it.*

"This book is the very best golf book that I have ever read...The best thing about the golf teachings in this book is that they really work.... an immediate and most profound impact on my game.... my scores dropped immediately!"

-Steve Justein,
Tournament Chairman,
Oakdale Golf & Country Club,
Toronto, Ontario.

Golf Is A Very Simple Game:
The Golf Teachings of the Late Señor Francisco Lopez Vol I.
IS AVAILABLE AT BOOK STORES AND GOLF SHOPS

WHAT'S THIS GOT TO DO WITH GOLF?

The Golf Teachings of the Late Señor Francisco Lopez Vol. II

ABOUT What's THIS Got to Do With GOLF?
The Golf Teachings of the Late Señor Francisco Lopez Vol II.

Two days after his golf pro and friend Frank Lopez died, author Jonathan Fine saw a satiny, gossamer-like cloud of energy pulsating near an electrical outlet. Feeling an eerie and powerful presence, Fine candidly admits that he believes this was Frank!

"Jonathan Fine, with the inspiration of the late Señor Francisco Lopez has done it again! *Golf Is A Very Simple Game* and now *What's THIS Got To Do With GOLF?* - both volumes are a MUST read for everyone, not just golfers. *THESE ARE THE THOUGHTS OF CHAMPIONS.* Valuable lessons on and off the golf course. BELIEVE IT! TRUST IT! READ IT!"

-Marlene Stewart Streit O.C.
Only woman ever to win the amateur championships
of United States, Canada, Britain, and Australia;
2-time U.S. Senior Ladies' Amateur Champion

Shortly thereafter, more weird things began happening to Fine, both on and off the golf course, but best of all, Fine's golf *improved dramatically*. Citing the incredible power of belief, Fine explains that whether Lopez' spirit actually helped Fine play better golf is irrelevant to him, attributing his success to *the belief* that it did.

> "A great sequel to *Golf Is A Very Simple Game*. A golf book with no swing mechanics is a breakthrough for golfers who want to take their games to a higher level. I RECOMMEND *What's THIS Got To Do With GOLF?* to all levels of golfers. Constant reading with an open mind *will* produce results!"
>
> -Cathy Sherk
> Former LPGA Tour player;
> U. S. and Canadian Amateur Champion;
> 3-time CPGA Ladies' Champion;
> 1978 *Golf Digest* top female golfer in the world

As in *Golf Is a Very Simple Game*, Mr. Fine's internationally acclaimed first book in this series about the *Golf Teachings of the Late Señor Francisco Lopez*, the reader soon realizes that *What's THIS Got To Do With GOLF?* is also as much a book of life lessons as golf lessons - and perhaps even more.

> "As a motivational coach, I am constantly on "demon patrol"- see chapter 91. Chapter 58 is awesome too!"
>
> -Pauline Kelly,
> Motivational Coach and
> Former All- American Golf Team Member

I n *What's THIS Got To Do With GOLF?*, Fine goes beyond the mental aspect of the game of golf and explores that *unique, spiritual, mystical and mystifying thing about the game of golf* which is at the juncture where the physical, metaphysical, conscious and subconscious meet. Being constantly challenged to break through the mental shell created by a closed mind and cynicism about unproven, perhaps even outrageous ideas, the reader asks over and over *"What's THIS got to do with GOLF"*, only to be gently directed to the answer.

"Most golfers have experienced the metaphysical side of golf: that unique, spiritual, mystical and mystifying thing about the game of golf that Frank Lopez called "IT." *Have you?* Golfers who continually excel however, go beyond simple awareness of IT and tap into this energy source and use IT. "

-Ben Jackson, Golf Professional,
Stonington C.C.,
Stonington Connecticut

"..this book will impact all levels of golfers...however, this book is not only for golfer, but is a great resource for anyone trying to achieve."

-John Novosel,
Inventor of the "Excelerator" and
President Sports Revolution Inc.

"This book offers what most "help related" books don't: how to physically and mentally prepare and perform. I particularly liked chapter 67. The message is clear: *"Think Good. Feel Good. Be Good. Be Good Feel Good. Think Good."*

-Ron Heller
Producer and Host of TV's *"Golf Is Our Game"*

Following the style of *Golf Is a Very Simple Game*, *What's THIS Got To Do With GOLF?* contains short, punchy chapters with specially chosen graphics on each page to accent visually, the point made by the text. A great read and a great philosophy of golf and life.

"...You got "IT". .... This book is as important in life as it is in golf, but then you and I know that there is no difference."

-Dudley Jones
Head Professional
Lambton Golf & Country Club
Toronto, Ontario

"Jonathan Fine has taken the mental approach of golf to the next level."

-Steven Justein
Tournament Chairman
Oakdale Golf & Country Club
Toronto, Ontario

What's THIS Got to Do With GOLF?
The Golf Teachings of the Late Señor Francisco Lopez
Vol II.
IS AVAILABLE
AT BOOK STORES AND GOLF SHOPS